QUARTERBLACK
Shattering the NFL Myth

Doug Williams
with Bruce Hunter

Bonus Books, Inc. Chicago

94 93 92 91 90   5 4 3 2

International Standard Book Number: 0-929387-47-3

Library of Congress 90-83207

Bonus Books, Inc.
160 East Illinois Street
Chicago, Illinois 60611

Printed in the United States of America

*Special thanks to Bertha Faye Thomas for suggesting Quarterblack
as the book title.*

In memory of my late wife, Janice, and my daddy, Robert Williams, Sr.

Contents

Preface

Growing up in a small town like Zachary, Louisiana, during the mid-1960s, I never imagined I would someday have the opportunity to have a book written about my life and the people and events that influenced it. Although I've never thought of myself as a trailblazer, in some ways it has turned out that way.

Many people were influential in making me the kind of person I am today. My family, particularly my oldest brother Robert, who played minor league baseball but suffered a career ending injury to his throwing arm; my parents, to whom I owe a debt I can never repay; Eddie Robinson, my college football coach; Buddy and Linda Foster, who befriended me when I went to Tampa and stood by me during the death of my first wife, Janice, and the contract hassle with the Tampa Bay Buccaneers; and other professional athletes such as Muhammad Ali and Kareem Abdul-Jabbar.

Out of the many experiences I've had during my career, the most rewarding and satisfying is being able to share with others, especially young people, the benefits of my accomplishments through the efforts of such organizations as the Doug Williams Foundation. Also, to show by example that through hard work, dedication, and patience they can do whatever they set their minds to.

During the last several years I have likened myself and my career to that of people such as the late Martin Luther King, Jr., Jackie Robinson, and Jesse Owens who had to overcome major obstacles to gain some measure of respect in their professions and recognition for their achievements. My one desire has always been to be known as a quarterback, like the Terry Bradshaws, Joe Montanas, Dan Fouts, and many others in the NFL. But instead they color me ''Quarterblack.''

Doug Williams
July 1990

Redskins Farewell

Like most days last spring, I got up early on the morning of March 28 and drove my seven-year-old daughter, Ashley, to school. Then I went right to the office behind my house in Zachary, Louisiana, and worked out on the treadmill and weights. I had a football season ahead of me.

There were only three days left in the Plan B free agent signing period, and I expected to return to the Washington Redskins. I was looking forward to the 1990 season, even though Redskins coach Joe Gibbs had announced Mark Rypien would be our starting quarterback. We had a talented group of veterans, most of whom were a part of our Super Bowl victory in 1988, and I thought we had a good chance to get back in the playoffs and make a run at another championship.

This was going to be my tenth season in the National Football League, five with the Tampa Bay Buccaneers and five with the Redskins. At Tampa Bay, we made it to the NFC championship game in my second season and only the fourth year of the franchise. No other expansion team in history has been so successful so soon. In my years with the Redskins, we had been to two NFC championship games and won a Super Bowl. I wanted to finish my career with another championship. I wanted to finish my career with the Redskins.

All that changed with one phone call. After my workout that morning, I checked my answering machine and there was a message to call Coach Gibbs. When we finally got in touch with each other that afternoon, I could tell right away something was up, because there was a strange sound to his voice.

"Douglas, I need to see you," he said in a very businesslike way. "I have to talk to you face to face."

Having been around Coach Gibbs for so many years, both at Tampa Bay and Washington, I could sense there was a problem. I suspected something was going to happen that probably wasn't what I wanted. I told him that I had to be in Washington on Friday the thirtieth, so we agreed to meet at Redskins Park.

In the meantime, I thought a lot about his tone of voice and what he said to me. It was on my mind all day and all night on Wednesday and Thursday. Then I thought about it some more on the flight to Washington. I had a good idea what was going to happen to me.

Toward the end of the 1989 season, I could tell my days as the starting quarterback for the Redskins were over. Coach Gibbs made it clear that he was going to go with Rypien as the starter. But I had no problem with that. I had shown that I could accept being the backup, and I had proven that I could be effective coming off the bench. After all, the Redskins signed me to be the backup in 1986, and I was still the backup at the start of our Super Bowl season.

Even though I had just come off back surgery, I had played some late in the 1989 season and played well. My health was not a factor. Neither was my age. I was going to turn thirty-five before the start of the season, but there have been plenty of quarterbacks play in the NFL who were older than that. Much older. Besides, I knew Coach Gibbs likes to have a veteran quarterback around just in case. In the past, he's signed Jim Hart, Steve Bartkowski and Jeff Kinney as back-ups.

I had not been surprised when the Redskins didn't protect me in February under Plan B. It just didn't make sense to put me on the Plan B protected list. Here's a thirty-five-year-old quarterback who is making $1.2 million, who has just recently had back surgery and who has played for Joe Gibbs at two different places. A lot of people around the league figured I was going to stay with the Redskins. So why should they protect me? I knew I was going to be a Plan B free agent.

I've been around the league long enough to know how things work. Nobody had to tell me.

What did surprise me was the lack of interest from other teams once I became a Plan B free agent. There were a lot of teams that needed a quarterback. The New Orleans Saints certainly needed help. They had Bobby Hebert, who said he'd never play for them again, and John Fourcade, who was never good enough to play for anybody until the Saints got desperate late in the 1989 season. It would have been nice to finish my career in my home state. But I knew it wouldn't happen. The Saints had a chance to get me five different times during my career and never once contacted me.

I did expect to get some serious contacts from other teams. My agent, Brigg Owens, got calls from the Cleveland Browns and New York Giants, but they weren't seriously interested at the time. Maybe if they lost somebody, they would have come back to talk to me. But no team was willing to make an offer.

Actually, that helped me prepare for what was to come. I really wanted to play another season for the Redskins, and I expected to get that opportunity. Yet at the same time, I realized there was a chance I might not play again. There's always that chance in professional sports.

When I went in to see Coach Gibbs on Friday, I was prepared to hear the fact that I was no longer going to be a Redskin. That helped me keep my emotions under control. Usually, when it comes to dealing with my career and my livelihood, I have a tendency to get emotional. But not this time.

Going into the Redskins office, I was my usual self, smiling and greeting everyone I saw. I stopped and spoke to several people, and finally worked my way to Coach Gibbs' office.

As usual, Coach Gibbs got up and made me feel welcome. He asked, "How have you been, Douglas? How's the family?" We sat down and started a friendly conversation.

Then Coach Gibbs got to the point.

"I've been thinking about this for a long time," he said reflectively. "It's been on my mind for weeks. We've had four good years together here. We've had a lot of good times. Remember 1987 when I sat right here and said I didn't want to trade you to the Raiders because I thought you were going to help us win the championship. We got that Super Bowl ring, didn't we? And you've overcome so many things here. I think we've made the complete cycle.''

I could tell Coach Gibbs didn't want to say he was releasing me. Knowing him like I do and having been friends with him for so long, I knew he would have a hard time saying it was over. He wanted me to stop him and say, ''Coach, I think it's best for me to go on and retire.'' But I wasn't going to retire, knowing that I'm still capable of playing for the Redskins or any other team in the league.

Then Coach Gibbs talked about being worried about my health. I appreciated his concern for my well being, and I believe it was genuine. I've always thought Coach Gibbs was a fair man. At least as fair as he could be in this league. But as a football player, you know you take certain risks, and I was willing to take them. My back felt fine. I had been working out to get ready for mini-camp. I wanted to play.

''Douglas, I've decided to go with the younger guys,'' Coach Gibbs said definitively. ''I feel if we're going to go anywhere, it's going to be with the young guys. And I wouldn't enjoy the idea of coaching you as the backup or third-teamer. I couldn't face you in meetings. It wouldn't be fair to you after all you've done.''

There didn't seem to be much point in saying anything. The decision clearly had been made. Finally, I told him, ''I did not come in here to try to convince you that I can still play. I know you've already made up your mind. If that's the case, then just go on and release me.''

''Do you want me to wait awhile before we let the news out?'' Coach Gibbs asked.

''No, just do it today. Let's get it over with.''

I guess Coach Gibbs had forgotten that I had spent most of my years with the Redskins as a backup. Besides, football is my profession. We were talking about my livelihood, and I didn't appreciate him making the decision for me.

Coach Gibbs said he didn't want to put me in a position of being inactive. Well, let me make that choice for myself. That should have been my decision to make.

All I wanted was another chance to prove myself. My career has been one of always having to prove myself. I was ready for another challenge. If I didn't make the team in training camp, that was fine. Then they could cut me. But as it turned out, they didn't even give me a shot.

Then came the clincher. Coach Gibbs told me, "We're going to sign the best available quarterback. That's Jeff Rutledge."

That really shocked me. I couldn't believe they were going to bring in somebody like Rutledge from the Giants. This is a guy who has never done anything in the league. He's hardly even played. At that point, I was hurt, I was embarrassed, and I was angry. I couldn't hold back any longer.

"Coach, I'm going to tell you like it is," I said, staring at him eye to eye. "I don't think a healthy Jeff Rutledge could beat out a banged-up Doug Williams!"

Coach Gibbs didn't respond to that. After all, what could he say? He knows Rutledge can't play. And he said they're going with youth. Well, Rutledge is just a year younger than me.

That was about the end of the conversation. It had lasted no more than fifteen minutes. I got up, shook his hand and left. I could have said a lot more, but I did not.

Coach Gibbs told the press that it was an emotional meeting. I think he got emotional, but I didn't. I refused to let myself get emotional. I wasn't going to go out like that.

Actually, the main reason they let me go was to save money. No doubt about it, this was a business decision. My contract called for $1.2 million for the 1990 season, and they signed Rutledge for about $300,000. That's a $900,000 savings. Coach Gibbs said it wasn't a business move, but how can you ignore the facts? I'll probably go to my grave thinking it was a business decision, not a football decision.

They didn't even give me a choice of taking a pay cut or retiring. I guess they were afraid I wouldn't take the cut, and then they'd have a controversy.

A lot of prominent people in Washington called me and said it was a matter of the Redskins trying to avoid a quarterback controversy. Suppose Rypien and Stan Humphries, the Redskins other quarterback, weren't playing well, and I was sitting on the sidelines again. Then we'd start hearing the old chant: "We Want Doug! We Want Doug!" And Coach Gibbs hates that kind of controversy. He can't stand it.

Coach Gibbs probably thought it would be easier to eliminate that possibility before the season than to let it drag on. It's easy to forget someone, especially if your team is playing well. Winning makes you forget everything else. But if the Redskins don't win and the quarterbacks don't perform, they're still going to say, "You should have kept Doug."

I believe it was a combination of finances and avoiding controversy. Unfortunately, it seems that wherever I've been, I've been involved in controversy. Black quarterbacks are always going to be controversial in the NFL.

The thing the Redskins didn't take into consideration is what I meant to the team. Here's an inspirational leader of the team. Someone who has led them to the Super Bowl. Someone who is actively involved in the community. Someone who represents the organization well in many capacities. You can't replace those things. From that standpoint, they made a major mistake.

Leaving Redskins Park that day was the hard part for me. I did get emotional saying good-bye to the secretaries like Pat White, Barbara Frye, Rita Martin, Kelly Peucker, and Phyllis Hayes in the P.R. Dept. Then I talked to Jay Brunetti, the equipment manager; Donnie Schoenmann, the film man; and some of my teammates who were there working out. It was over for me. I wasn't coming back. I was no longer a Redskin.

My teammates didn't believe me at first. But I told them, "Yeah, it's true. I'm through here." I don't think they really believed the Redskins released me until it was on TV and in the papers. A lot of them called me at home the next day.

The call that meant the most was from Jeff Bostic. We had gone through a lot together. When I first came to the Redskins, they had said Jeff wasn't big enough to play center, and they wanted to find a 300-pound lineman to defeat the New York Giants. They took away his starting job and put him on the sidelines with me. So we started calling ourselves the B team. Then when the Redskins were talking about trading me to the Raiders, we joked that we probably would be going together as a package deal. Jeff eventually got his starting job back, then I moved up to starting quarterback, and we won the Super Bowl. Not bad for the B team.

"This is the other part of the B team," Jeff said when he called. "And I just want to let you know whatever we can do for you we will. We're going to be here rooting for you. I know you can still do it."

Jeff told the papers that I still have some football left in me. I know that better than anyone. I could have played another year or two.

Maybe longer. On draft day, Mel Kiper said on ESPN that I have several good years left to play and the Raiders should sign me. Maybe they will, or perhaps I'll go somewhere else. But I won't be surprised if nobody picks me up.

What it comes down to is black quarterbacks rarely get a chance to sit around and make money as backups in the NFL. It's part of the black quarterback syndrome that has plagued the league since its inception. A lot of NFL coaches, general managers and owners either don't want a black man in a leadership role such as quarterback or they just don't want to buck the system, which says a black man isn't capable of handling the position. As a result, the backup quarterback position in the NFL is for white players only. Blacks need not apply.

Just look around the league. Don McPherson of the Philadelphia Eagles and rookie Andre Ware of Detroit are the only black backup quarterbacks left in the NFL. When James Harris was finishing up his career with the San Diego Chargers, he would have been a valuable backup quarterback for some team. But nobody would keep him around. And now it's happened to me.

There are plenty of veteran quarterbacks still playing in the NFL. There's Don Strock. He's forty, and he played for Indianapolis last year. Ron Jaworski is thirty-nine, and he played for Kansas City last year. Joe Ferguson is forty, and he played for the Bucs. Steve Grogan is thirty-eight, and he's still starting for the Patriots.

So am I too old at thirty-five? That's not the problem. The fact is NFL teams are not going to pay a black quarterback unless he is definitely going to play. I really thought the Redskins were above that. But even they weren't willing to pay a black quarterback to be a backup. That's not an opinion, it's a sad fact.

One day after my release, the headline in the *Washington Post* read: "(No) Thanks For The Memories." And Michael Wilbon closed his column in the *Post* with this: "Doug Williams did good for the Washington Redskins. Maybe too good. Maybe they didn't deserve him."

I can't say the Redskins didn't deserve Doug Williams. But I can say Doug Williams deserved a better farewell from the Redskins.

2

Super Sunday

The first rays of sunlight danced through the bedroom window of the luxurious condominium. Outside, the early birds were beginning to descend upon the golf course which weaved its green way through the Lawrence Welk Resort. Even without looking out the window, I could tell it was going to be one of those brilliant, cloudless days in the California desert. So beautiful that I wanted to get some clubs and go join the golfers for a leisurely eighteen holes.

My assignment for the day was not so relaxing. Certainly, not as carefree. Definitely, not so insignificant. This was the day I had waited for all my life, that black America had anticipated for decades. I was starting at quarterback for the Washington Redskins, and that afternoon, we were playing the Denver Broncos in Super Bowl XXII in San Diego's Jack Murphy Stadium.

It was January 31, 1988, and they had been playing professional football for more than sixty years. Yet, there had never been a black quarterback in the league championship game. I guess a lot of people in the NFL thought there never would be, or at least hoped there never would be. It had taken me ten years of fighting the league's prejudice toward playing black quarterbacks to get this far.

Hundreds of millions of people across the globe would be watching me. I had woken up at 6:00 or 6:30, but that wasn't even early enough. I didn't want to miss anything. Not a thing. When you talk about Super Sunday, I wanted to get it all. When the sun came up, I wanted to be up with it. When it went down, I wanted to see it. I was tired of waiting for the game. I was tired of all the hype that goes along with the Super Bowl. I wanted to play. If they had wanted to kick off at eight o'clock in the morning, I would have been ready to play. Whatever happened, I was ready for it.

As I laid on my back and stared at the ceiling, the first thing that crossed my mind was that the pain from my toothache had disappeared. I couldn't believe it. On Saturday, we had a barbecue after practice, and my tooth started killing me. So I went to see the team dentist, Dr. Barry Rudolph. He took me to a dental office in the suburbs of San Diego and found out I needed a root canal.

"Doc, a root canal?" I pleaded, trying not to believe this was happening to me less than twenty-four hours before the Super Bowl. "This is Saturday. We've got to play tomorrow. How can I have a root canal now?"

"Doug, it's better to take care of it now than let it go and find out tomorrow it's too painful," Dr. Rudolph responded.

"All right, Doc. You know what you're doing. Let's get it done."

The root canal took about four hours. I can't be any more precise than that because Dr. Rudolph put me asleep. When I woke up, I was in extreme pain. All I wanted to do was take something to make it stop hurting and go to bed. Back at the team hotel, the San Diego Marriott, everyone was asking, "Where's Doug? Where's Doug?" Dr. Rudolph had called Coach Gibbs and team owner Jack Kent Cooke. But they were the only ones who knew about it.

When I finally returned to the hotel, I had to pack an overnight bag because Coach Gibbs wanted to move the team to another location. He didn't want us around all the commotion the night before the Super Bowl. Nobody had any idea where we were going. It didn't matter to me anyway. I just wanted the soreness in my mouth to go away.

We drove on a bus out into the desert. About an hour out of the city, we finally came to the Lawrence Welk Resort, which is located in a place called Escondido, California. Although it's one of the most comfortable condos I've ever stayed in, that night it really didn't matter. I went straight to bed. All I wanted was some Perkadan and some sleep.

It was amazing when I woke up with no pain. None at all. It was hard to believe that I could have been hurting so much Saturday and then have no pain Sunday morning. All I could do was chalk it up to the fact Dr. Rudolph did a wonderful job. I was feeling so good. I stayed in bed for about an hour just thinking about a lot of things that popped into my mind.

There was plenty of time left before we had to go to the pregame meal. We always ate four hours before the game. The Super Bowl was scheduled to start at 3:00 p.m. on the West Coast. During those early morning hours, I just put my whole career in front of me. I thought about plays and incidents that had an impact on me getting there.

My mind raced through my childhood days in Zachary, Louisiana, and then those five years I spent with legendary Grambling coach Eddie Robinson, who shaped my way of thinking and helped me develop into a Heisman Trophy finalist and become the first black quarterback to be selected in the first round of the NFL draft.

Then I reflected on what I had done in five years with the Tampa Bay Buccaneers. Three playoff berths, two NFC Central Division championships and one berth in the NFC championship game. I believed we were on the verge of getting to the Super Bowl in 1982, but Bucs owner Hugh Culverhouse showed his true colors. After five years as a starter, I was the fifty-fourth highest paid quarterback in the league and had never even asked to renegotiate my contract. Culverhouse wanted me to be his slave. I think he would have been the perfect slave owner.

Culverhouse tried to take advantage of me with some bogus real estate deal. I know Culverhouse didn't want a black quarterback, and a lot of the Tampa fans didn't either, but the Bucs had been 0-26 before I got there and they were willing to do anything to win. Finally, I realized Culverhouse was never going to pay me what I deserved, so I had to leave. At the same time that was going on, my wife Janice was diagnosed with a brain tumor and died a week later. I had a three-month-old daughter to raise, so I almost quit playing football altogether. But then the USFL started up, and I played two seasons in that league before it folded.

I decided I didn't want to think about Hugh Culverhouse on Super Sunday. It was my day. Instead, I turned my thoughts to the Washington Redskins. I considered how fortunate I was to be with Washington and to have the opportunity that I had. The Redskins are a class organization from owner Jack Kent Cooke all the way down the line. They were strong enough to give me a second chance in the NFL when no other team would contact me. I found out that the Bucs tried to blackball me from returning to the league. But the Redskins didn't listen to Culverhouse and his flunky, Phil Krueger. I appreciated the Redskins' loyalty. I wanted to reward them with a Super Bowl victory.

Even after I was wide awake, I still didn't want to get up. There was so much on my mind. I went over all the good, the bad and the ugly that had happened to me. I could have quit football. I could have gone a different direction in my life. I could have wound up on drugs, but I never gave in to drugs or anything else. I don't smoke or drink. A lot of it has to do with a person's will. You have to be a leader and not a follower. I'm the type of person who expects people to do what I do, not just what I say. That's being a leader, not a follower. People who are followers don't last long. You've got to do what's good for yourself. You've got to stand up for yourself and others. That's what being a leader is.

Later on, I began to think about the game itself. I just thanked God that I made it that far and overcame so many things to get that opportunity. All week I had to deal with being black. The media kept hyping me as the first black quarterback to play in the Super Bowl. That's all they ever wanted to talk about. They treated John Elway as a quarterback they respected. But they just wanted to see me as a black quarterback. All week I fought off being black.

Then all of a sudden, it was game day, and I was black again. I realized, "Hey, when I run through the chute, I'm going to be the first black quarterback to ever play in the Super Bowl." That was the first time I had really put it in my mind: "This is a reality. This is the truth. Doug Williams, you're the first black to play quarterback in the Super Bowl." I wondered how many people in America would be pulling for Doug Williams and how many people in America would be pulling against Doug Williams. I wasn't really sure what to expect. I knew there were plenty of people in the NFL who didn't want me in the Super Bowl, much less winning it.

Reading the newspaper clippings all week, I was supposed to think I didn't have a prayer. I mean I was just expected to show up, be the black quarterback and go home. It was John Elway's Super Bowl. He had been there the year before and lost to the New York Giants, but now he was going to take it out on the Redskins. The game belonged to him.

Fortunately for me, I knew that I had some people on my side. The Hogs were the best offensive line in football, and we had three great receivers in Ricky Sanders, Art Monk and Gary Clark. I was glad I didn't have to go in there by myself. And I had a feeling that Elway was going to try to do it by himself. I brought my team along with me. I knew that would be the difference. I was confident, and so was our team.

I've watched Elway for a long time, and I've seen some of the best quarterbacks play the game. But I haven't seen too much that they could do or have done that I couldn't do or haven't done. I used to be a scrambler, too. Nobody could scramble better than me when I was at Tampa. And I think I can throw the ball with the best of them. So I never believed that Elway or "No Way" was better than me. I wasn't going to concede that to anybody. I refused to tell myself John Elway was better than Doug Williams. My career has been a career of proof anyway. Look what we had accomplished at Tampa. No other expansion team has had that much success so early. When I did things like that, they always wanted to find excuses why I did it or they wrote or said, "He couldn't do it again." Well, I did it again, and more, with the Redskins. Now the media was giving it to Elway. But I wasn't. I knew what I was capable of, not as a black quarterback, but as the quarterback of the Washington Redskins.

As it got closer to the time for our pregame meal, I turned on the television set, watched some cartoons and made a couple phone calls. I watch cartoons every Saturday and Sunday. Some kids never grow up. I especially love the old ones like Bugs Bunny. I'm a cartoon man.

I always called my Dad before every game and then after the game, too. He was the first person I wanted to talk to that morning. The rest of my family had come to San Diego. There were twenty-two altogether. Daddy had rheumatoid arthritis and was in a wheelchair, so he didn't come. But I had to speak to him before this game.

"You hang in there, Doug," Daddy encouraged me as usual. "How are you feeling today?"

"I'm fine, Daddy. I had a root canal yesterday, but I'm all right now."

"Son, just remember to pray about the game. It's going to be all right."

Daddy wasn't what you would call a strict religious person. He wasn't in church all the time. But he believed in God. And he knew prayers would change things.

"Whatever happens, Doug, just remember you did your best," Daddy said before hanging up.

My father always did his best for our family. Even though Daddy was a disabled veteran from World War II, he kept working all of his life. He gave us a lot of discipline and taught us to believe in ourselves and believe in God.

Just to get a little more positive reinforcement, I picked up the phone again and called a close friend of mine by the name of Sharon Moore. We actually met while I was student teaching at Grambling State University and she was attending Grambling High School. I taught one of her classes, and we've kept in touch through the years.

Sharon is a very vivacious, positive person. That's why I called her. She was finishing up medical school at the University of Pittsburgh and had gone through some tough times. When she needed a boost, she called me. When I was on a downer, I called her. We just helped each other that way.

"Williams, I was hoping you would call," Sharon said, calling me by my last name as is her custom. "I prayed for you last night. I know God is going to be with you. I know you're going to be all right."

Like always, she kept building me up with encouragement. Sharon is a real good friend that way. We didn't talk long, but our conversation really had an impact. I was more anxious than ever to get to the stadium, and more certain that this would be the Redskins' day. And mine, too.

Once I finally left the condo to go to the pregame meal, the sun had filled the sky with its radiance and warmed the air to a comfortable temperature. I walked to the resort's cafeteria and ate a light brunch. A small steak and some fruit juice. That's about all I usually eat before a game. I don't believe you can eat a lot and then go out and play your best. I never want to feel sluggish or get sick, particularly on an occasion like this.

The team buses left the complex about noon and headed back to the city. Traffic was picking up, so it took a little over an hour to get to Jack Murphy Stadium. I had never set eyes on the place before that afternoon. It's just an average looking stadium, nothing impressive about it.

What I remember most was driving up to the stadium and seeing all the fans lining the streets and tailgating in the parking lot. As I looked out the window of the bus, I started to get air in my stomach. There were butterflies galore. I usually don't get nervous at all until I put on my uniform. But this was entirely different. This game was for the Super Bowl championship, and I knew the world would be watching me. History was about to be made, and I was going to make it. It was sinking in that I would be part of history, no matter what happened.

Even if I wasn't going to be the first black quarterback, this was still the Super Bowl. For a professional football player, this is it. It doesn't get any bigger. This is the pinnacle. You know when you sign that first contract, you're going to get paid for the job. But after a while you want those diamonds on your fingers. You get your ass knocked around enough that you realize a Super Bowl ring is what you need to make it all worthwhile. Out of all the injuries, pain and heartaches I've been through, it was all worth it knowing that I would be looking at a ring. That says you have been there. From a contentment standpoint, there is nothing like it. There are a lot of players in the Hall of Fame who don't have a ring. Heck, Joe Namath has only one ring. And I was about to get one for myself.

Inside our locker room, I could sense the other guys felt the significance of the game. Of course, most of the veterans on our team had been to the Super Bowl and won it. So even though we were intense, there weren't any worried faces. Just the opposite, everyone was walking around talking to someone. Maybe just patting them on the shoulder and saying, "Have a good one." Other guys sat and discussed what they had done all week and the people they had met.

I like a noisy locker room. To me, if it's quiet enough to hear a rat piss on cotton, that's not a good situation. I don't like teams like that. I want to tell them, "If you're scared, call the police. Don't go out there with me if you're scared." That was never a problem with the Redskins. We were a very confident team.

Everyone was relaxed and calm and expressing themselves. No one was getting carried away, except Dexter Manley. You have to expect that. He got taped and put this hot stuff all over his body and greased himself up. Then he walked up and down the locker room breathing heavy and getting himself psyched up. Coach Gibbs doesn't like loud, boastful players. But that's just Dexter, and you can't keep him from being himself.

You could tell everyone was enjoying this day and we felt we were going to win the game. You could just feel the confidence in that room. The media didn't give us a chance. They were giving it to Elway and the Broncos. But that just made us all the more determined. We knew we had a team. We really worked together. That week, we had had the best practices of the season, so we never had a doubt about our abilities. Our strength was the offensive and defensive lines, and we believed we were going to control the trenches. If you do that, you're going to win the game.

I waited until the kickers and a few other players had gone out on the field before I went out to warmup. I never wanted to be the first one out for warmups. That's just something I have never liked, all those people looking at you. I went out with K.B., which is what we call Kelvin Bryant. We've always been tight, but I don't refer to him as my best friend. For me, it isn't right to single out one person as your best friend. I wanted to get along with everybody on the team, and I think I had a good relationship with all my teammates on the Redskins, except my backup, Jay Schroeder. But that wasn't my fault. Schroeder didn't have many friends on the team, none that I knew about anyway.

There was nothing special about warmups, even though it was the Super Bowl. The stadium was still half empty, and there wasn't a lot of attention on us. My arm felt good, but it always feels good in warmups. I'm the type of person that I expect to have a big day every time I play. The only thing I didn't like about warmups was the time schedule. They came earlier than usual because the pregame show would be long. When we went back into the locker room, we still had a half hour to wait. That's a long time to just sit there, especially after you had an hour to get ready for warmups. We just talked some more, and the offense got together and called our first play. It was 40 Lead Nose, a basic trap play up the middle to our tailback. We thought we could dominate the line of scrimmage and that would be a good way to set the tone for the game.

When we finally lined up for the introductions, we were told the offensive players would be introduced over the public address system. That meant my name would be called and millions of people would be watching on TV when I ran out of the chute.

While waiting for my name, I was nervous. But I still wanted to hear Doug Williams being announced as the Redskins quarterback. In those final moments, what I tried to do was consider myself like any other warm-blooded, black American. I wanted to be proud of Doug Williams playing in the Super Bowl. I tried to put myself in the position of any other black American. If Randall Cunningham or Warren Moon had been playing, I would have been proud. I would have wished it was me, but I still would have been proud. I remember Moon wrote in some newspaper that he wished he had been the first black quarterback to play in the Super Bowl, and I'm sure I would have felt that way. But at the same time, I wanted to try to put me, being myself, on the side and try to be just one black American saying I witnessed Doug Williams play in the Super Bowl. I didn't want to involve myself as a player in the matter of being a black quarterback in the Super Bowl. That's what I wanted to do anyway. But no matter how I tried to approach it, I was still Doug Williams and that was going to be me out there.

When I heard my name called and started to run on the field, I thought about two guys, "Jefferson Street" Joe Gilliam and James Harris. They were the first black quarterbacks to have some success in the league, and I have a lot of respect for them. I really think they made it a lot easier for me. So I wasn't going to play just for me. I was going to play for Joe, James, Vince Evans, who combined with me to be the first two black quarterbacks to oppose each other in an NFL game when he was with the Bears and I was with the Bucs, and myself. I figured Randall and Warren could take care of themselves.

We got the ball first, but couldn't move it and had to punt. Then on their first offensive play of the game, Elway threw a touchdown pass to Ricky Nattiel. So we were down 7-0. Then we stunk up the joint in the next couple of offensive series, too. Our running plays weren't going anywhere. We dropped a couple of passes. One of them would have been a first down, but Gary Clark didn't make the easy catch. We missed a block or two, and I got hit. Nothing was going right early. We punted twice, and the next thing we knew we were down 10-0.

Falling behind didn't bother us at all. What people had forgotten was we were down 14-0 just three weeks earlier playing Chicago in the freezing cold. We had the type of team that wasn't bothered by being behind. We always knew we could come back. We still expected to dominate the game. It was too early to start worrying.

On our third series, things got a little more serious. I dropped back to pass and slipped on a wet spot on the grass. They had watered the field, and the part that was in the shade didn't dry all the way. As soon as I slipped, I could feel the pain shooting into my left knee. That was real pain. The worst kind of pain. Pain galore. I thought, "Lord, don't let this happen to me now. Please not now."

As I was helped to the sideline and Schroeder came in to take my place, I was hurting but still had a good feeling about it. I knew if there wasn't anything torn to the point I couldn't walk, I would come back. I had to get back in there. I had led us to the Super Bowl with those playoff wins over Minnesota and Chicago, and I felt I was the one to lead us to the championship.

We ran two plays while they were checking me on the bench, and then had to punt the ball. The first quarter was almost over when the Broncos got the ball. Our defense held and forced them to punt it back. Their punt came on the first play of the second quarter, and we got the ball on our 20. I told Coach Gibbs that I was ready to go back in. Coach Gibbs never said a word. He knew I would tell him if I couldn't play and he knew I would tell him if I was ready. We had a good relationship that way.

Once I got back in the game, my knee was throbbing, but it was all downhill from there. The first call was Charlie 10 Hitch. It's just an ordinary play where the quarterback takes a short drop and the receiver runs seven yards and just turns, unless the other team plays another defense. What the Broncos did was pressure us and play bump and run. So I read the coverage and the pattern automatically changed to an up route, where the receiver delays like he's going to turn and then takes off. Ricky Sanders put one heck of a move on Mark Haynes, and Haynes didn't get his hands on Ricky. Ricky was off to the races and was so wide open. The pass wasn't any more than twenty yards. We had thrown that pattern all year, so it was just reaction. I threw the ball where he could catch it, and it was just a matter of outrunning the safety, Tony Lilly. He had the angle on Ricky, but he didn't have the speed to get to him. I just watched Ricky outrun him and go all the way, eighty yards, for our first touchdown. We needed that in the worst way. That was the boost we really needed. We had to get something started. After we scored, our confidence level shot way up.

The defense really played hard and set the tempo for the offense. They got us the ball right back. We moved down to their 27. Then we caught the Broncos in a blitz, and Gary Clark was running a corner route. Ordinarily, it would have been a pass in the flats to K.B., but their linebacker was blitzing and didn't get to me, so I had time to look for Gary. It was man-on-man, and Gary just beat his man. Man, it was easy again. He caught the ball and fell into the end zone. That put us ahead for the first time, and I felt from a confidence standpoint we had it going and were finally about to take control of the football game.

Our defensive plan was working perfectly. We wanted to keep Elway in the pocket, make him read and make him throw. And he was having problems doing that. If he got outside the pocket, the way he could scramble, he could make things happen. But we weren't letting him do that.

Once again, our defense stopped them, and we were right back on the field. I handed off to Timmy Smith on a counter play, and he had a huge hole. Still, I was amazed that Lilly didn't tackle him. I didn't think Timmy could run that fast, and it looked like Lilly had the angle on him. But that day Timmy really ran well and went fifty-eight yards for a TD. And let me tell you, he had some big holes. Oh my gosh, they were such big holes. It wasn't even close.

Our front line just manhandled them. It was no contest for the Hogs. There was no doubt who was winning the war. We knew coming into the game that the Broncos were more of a finesse team. They beat a lot of teams with trickery—blitzing and mixing up different offenses and defenses. We knew that if it came down to man-on-man, we were the better team, and we were going to win.

The next time we got the ball, we were at midfield and faked the same run that Timmy had just scored on. The play was 60 Counter Cardinal, which is a play-action pass or run-pass as we call it. The fake just sucked the safety in again. Lilly was having a tough day. Ricky ran a post, and Lilly never got there. He wasn't even close. He took the bite on the run, and Ricky blew by him. I threw it to him again, and it was a quick six.

That put us ahead 28-10, and gave me three touchdown passes for the day. The stadium was really getting loud. I think the fans were pulling for me. It seemed like they wanted Doug Williams to have a good day for sentimental reasons. Everyone knew all the bullshit I had gone through with the media all week. They also knew my story, where I had come from and how I got to the Super Bowl. I think they were just ready to see a change in America. It seemed like they wanted to see a black man get a chance. They wanted to be there to watch Doug Williams help the Redskins win the Super Bowl. By then, we were in complete control. But with the things Elway was capable of doing, both throwing and running, you couldn't think you were going to win, because anything can happen.

Time was running out in the half, but we weren't going to be conservative. We called a timeout and talked things over. Then we produced a nice, long drive. Once we got inside the 10, we called Slick Left, which is a corner route for the tight end. Ricky faked motion, came back and went in the flat. He drew his guy up, and Clint Didier, our tight end, just went behind him to the corner. Clint killed his guy and was all alone in the end zone. I got the ball there and we had another TD. That made it 35-10, and we were flying. I didn't even care that my knee was killing me. Nothing mattered but beating the Broncos.

It was the most points ever scored in one quarter of the Super Bowl, and it was easy. It was like taking candy from a baby. That day, Denver did not do a good job of covering. You want to be in a position like that. Football has become such a computerized game that it's like cat and mouse. The cat is only going to catch the mouse every so often. We just happened to be the cat, and we had the mouse. The mouse did not have a chance. We felt from a strategy standpoint we had the upperhand. As a quarterback, there is no better feeling. You can do whatever you want in a situation like that, and they know it.

As we went to the locker room, I realized how much my knee hurt. I was in pain. Tremendous pain. All I could think about was getting something to stop the pain. I wouldn't have been enjoying myself anyway. As a competitive athlete, you never enjoy a game until it is over. That's the worst thing in the world you can do. Through the years, I have seen so many things happen. You never celebrate and you never enjoy the moment until it's all over. As the saying goes, it's not over until the fat lady sings. And the fat lady wasn't about to sing at halftime.

My mind was set on getting one of those good ol' novacaine shots. They wouldn't do that during the game, because they don't pull out those big needles on the sidelines for everyone to see.

In the locker room, Coach Joe Bugel, our offensive line coach and assistant head coach, walked up to me.

"Stud," Coach Bugel said, using the name he always calls me. "We can finish this if you don't want to. We can let Jay play the second half."

"No, Coach, I started this, and I'm going to finish it."

Coach Bugel just nodded and let me go into the training room. I told Dr. Robert Jackson, one of our team doctors, to give me a shot, so he did. There was no way I was going to let Jay Schroeder play that day. He would have been in for two quarters. No way. It was my day, and I was going to play. I didn't want Jay to have any part of it.

The bottom line is Jay Schroeder is a prima donna asshole. All week I could tell it was eating him up that we were playing in the Super Bowl and he wasn't going to get in. He already had a nasty attitude, and everyone noticed the way he was acting. Coach Gibbs even contemplated not activating him for the Super Bowl. I was told he thought about bringing Mark Rypien up for the game, because Schroeder's attitude was so bad. In practice, he had been so nonchalant. It looked like he didn't care about the game one way or another. Heck, he didn't care about the team. When I was the backup quarterback, I went about my business and tried to help the team anyway I could. Whereas, he portrayed a very selfish attitude. He was for Jay Schroeder and Jay Schroeder only. The other guys picked up on it, and they didn't like the way he was acting. They didn't want him around. All of them knew he was a selfish individual.

Coach Gibbs could have just said we were going to let me rest and put Jay in to finish the game. He could easily have done that. It was his decision to make, but he left it up to me. That's the kind of man he is. After I got the shot, I felt great. There was no more pain, and I was ready to get back out there. I walked up to Coach Gibbs and told him I was ready to go. That was all he needed to hear.

I wanted to score more points. Any quarterback would want to score more points in the Super Bowl. We wanted thirty-five more, and we might have done it. But you have to understand Coach Gibbs. It could have gotten out of hand, but Coach Gibbs is not that way. Besides, he is good friends with Denver coach Dan Reeves. He didn't want to run the score up on him. After the game, he shook hands and told Coach Reeves, "I'm sorry."

In a way, I understood what Coach Gibbs was doing. You respect a guy for doing something like that. But as a player, you don't think that way. You want to crush the other team. That's just the way of football. Coach Robinson used to tell us at Grambling, "Kill a gnat with a sledge hammer." We had the gnat right in sight, and I wanted to kill it. Never let up. No wasted motion. Just boom.

If we had gone out with the same open minded game plan, we could have scored in the fifties. We didn't call a lot of things we called in the first half. We were so conservative it was pathetic. I threw the ball only eight times in the second half. Eight times. We didn't change the game plan per se. We just didn't call the same plays we called in the first half. Basically, we ran the ball the rest of the day and didn't score again until the final minutes of the game.

Our defense completely controlled the second half. Barry Wilburn had a couple interceptions. Brian Davis got one. Dexter Manley and Charles Mann put a lot of pressure on Elway. I loved it. Any time the other team's quarterback is under pressure, I love it. I have been on so many teams where I got my ass knocked around and the other guy enjoyed a great day. I love to see it happen the other way. And it couldn't have come in a better situation. This was the Super Bowl, and everything was going our way.

I don't have anything against John Elway. I'm smart enough to realize this is America. I remember hearing Terry Bradshaw say one day when he was announcing a game that certain quarterbacks get all the endorsements. I think he was talking about Boomer Esiason. Bradshaw made the statement, "He's just what America likes: blond hair and blue eyes." I couldn't believe Terry Bradshaw made that statement on television. But he did. And it's true.

Standing on that sideline at the Super Bowl, I understood why Elway had gotten all the hype. He is what America wants. And the sooner you learn to accept it and deal with it, the better off you will be. I have adjusted to the fact that this is America, and I know how things are. You can't change them all. You just have to deal with it and be content. I have learned to be content with a lot of things.

Even though we weren't throwing the ball, it was 35-10 in the Super Bowl and I was having a good time. I still had not let up, but I was starting to enjoy myself. The shot had taken care of the pain. Everything felt good.

But I didn't start to celebrate until our last drive when Timmy scored his second touchdown to make it 42-10. Then they announced that I had been voted the most valuable player, and all the guys came up to me and patted me on the helmet. That's when it finally set in, "This is over. This is history. We are the Super Bowl champions."

Being the MVP of the Super Bowl is certainly an honor. But on that day, it wasn't something I had to have. If they had given it to Ricky, if they had given it to Timmy, if they had given five of them to our offensive linemen, it would have been fine with me. Ricky had almost 200 yards worth of receptions and two touchdowns. He could have won it. Timmy rushed for over 200 yards and two touchdowns. He could have won it. We had over 600 yards and six touchdowns, so the Hogs could have won it.

I had thrown for 340 yards and four touchdowns, most of it in the second quarter. So they decided I was the MVP. For me, the MVP was just icing on the cake. Winning the Super Bowl was the important thing. That was the cake.

Walking off the field, I felt like I wanted that moment to last forever. It was crazy. It was great. I remember raising my helmet up as I walked off. A lot of things were going through my mind. I was summing up the week when nobody gave me a chance. Really, if that helmet could have fit up some of the media's behinds, I would loved to have stuck it up there.

As I headed toward the locker room, I looked into the stands, but didn't recognize anyone. It seemed like everyone was cheering for us. Then I saw Coach Robinson standing under the goalposts. One of the NFL's attorneys, David Cornwell, had arranged for him to come on the field to congratulate me. I went right over and gave him a hug. Coach Rob was probably the most thrilled person there that day. He kept hugging me and getting emotional.

"I didn't think I'd live to see the day that one of my quarterbacks would win the Super Bowl," Coach Rob told me, choking on his words. "Doug, you don't realize the impact you made. You are Jackie Robinson today. You're the Jackie Robinson of football. You don't understand what I'm talking about. You had to live in Jackie Robinson's era to understand it. Then you would know what Jackie had to go through, and then you would understand what this means."

All I knew was how elated Coach Rob was right then. And that made me all the more ecstatic. He has seen so much happen in football. He has been such a big part of blacks getting a chance to play in the NFL. For someone who had coached so long and won more games than any other coach, Coach Rob was finally getting his reward. I was just happy to be there to share it.

Coach Rob came with me to the locker room. But before we could get off the field, the public relations lady from DisneyWorld came running up to me. She had been looking for me all over the field, because Elway and I had signed a deal with DisneyWorld. Whichever quarterback won the game was supposed to look into the CBS camera and say that he was going to DisneyWorld, and he would get paid $75,000. Well, I didn't give a darn about DisneyWorld or the money at that moment. I had the Super Bowl on my mind, and nothing else mattered.

Maureen, the Disney woman in charge, got real excited and started shouting, "Doug, Doug, the camera." So I turned around and said, "I'm going to DisneyWorld" and smiled for the camera. Then I turned and headed back toward the locker room with Coach Rob.

By the time we got there, the locker room was filled with our players and coaches and the media. The place was wild. Everyone was putting on Super Bowl champion hats and hugging each other. Even if there was a teammate that someone didn't like, he still got hugged. I guess Jay even got hugged. We had a great celebration.

Later, they called us to the press conference, and Coach Rob went with me there. They asked him questions, too. Other than that, it was basically about how it felt to be the first black quarterback in the Super Bowl. They were the same ol' questions that I had heard all week. All I could say was: "I didn't come here as a black quarterback. I came here as the Washington Redskins quarterback. You paint me any way you want to." I really didn't care what they wrote about me on that day. I knew it belonged to me, Coach Rob, and millions of other black Americans across the country.

Between that night and the press conference the next morning, I was interviewed dozens of times by reporters from all over the country. But the best interview was the one with Keith Jackson right after the game. It was live from the locker room. I was humble with him, like I tried to be with everyone. It wasn't like I was trying to say, "I told you so" or that type of thing. Keith asked me what it was like to be the underdog and then lead my team to a Super Bowl victory, and I told him it was basically a team effort, which it was. He asked me about all the hype of being a black quarterback, and I told him I was just the Redskins quarterback. And as Keith was finishing the interview, the thing that stands out the most to me is what he said at the very end, "Thank you, SIR."

What Keith said meant a lot to me, because I interpreted it to mean, "Here is a guy who went through all the bullshit all week and still kept his humility, and I think we owe him some respect." I think that was Keith's way of saying, "I respect you, Doug Williams." And it seemed he was trying to get across to Americans watching on TV that we should all respect Doug Williams.

3

The Myth

I was always taught that America is the land of opportunity for all men. Coach Robinson loved to tell his Grambling players, "If it can happen, it will happen in America." But obviously it's not happening for black quarterbacks.

In 1989 only four NFL teams had black quarterbacks. Randall Cunningham and Don McPherson played for the Philadelphia Eagles, Warren Moon was with the Houston Oilers, Rodney Peete played in Detroit, and I was with the Washington Redskins. That's a shame. I call it the black quarterback syndrome. The sad thing is it's 1990, and I don't see it getting any better.

What is the black quarterback syndrome? It boils down to the fact that most NFL coaches, general managers and owners are scared of black quarterbacks or they just don't want a black man running their team, period. They're afraid if they play a black quarterback and he doesn't pan out, they're going to be ridiculed by their peers. People around the league will say, "I told you that black guy couldn't play."

One thing you have to realize is how closely the league's owners and general managers are associated. It's a clique, and they don't want to be looked down upon by their buddies. So they take the easy way out. It's safe to play a white quarterback. If he doesn't play well, they'll just say, "He's still young. Let's give him time to mature."

And if he doesn't make it, they'll just push him aside and get another one.

It's not that easy with a black guy. A black quarterback is always going to stand out. Back when James Harris was with the Los Angeles Rams, they were playing the Dallas Cowboys in the 1975 playoffs, and Shack had a bad ankle. But they brought him off the bench anyway. He threw an interception that led to a Dallas touchdown, and the Rams pulled him right away. That was just one touchdown in a 37-7 win for the Cowboys. Still, the Rams management blamed Shack for losing the game, and he never played for them again. They had to find somebody to blame, so they picked on the black quarterback. They traded Shack to San Diego. You can't tell me that Pat Haden, the Rams other quarterback, was better than James Harris. That's a joke.

It's a simple matter of NFL management being afraid of the black quarterback embarrassing them. I talk to Randall Cunningham about it all the time. He tells me a lot of the problems that the Eagles have. I just tell him, "You've got to be patient. Some things you just can't say. You've got to let them go." I've made a career of letting things go. As a black quarterback, you have to do that, or you'll never survive in the NFL.

And Randall is going to learn that if he ever falls out of grace, if there ever comes a time when he can't do the things he's capable of doing now, he's going to become just a black quarterback. Now he's Randall Cunningham. He can do some great things. But a lot of people in the league would like to see him be a black quarterback again.

This past season, Bobby Beathard, who was our general manager at Washington and is now with the Chargers, tried to fit Randall into the black quarterback mold. Beathard told the media that Randall is one of the most overrated players in the league. How in the hell are you going to say Randall Cunningham is overrated? If the Philadelphia Eagles don't have Randall, they don't win. It's that simple. Beathard knows enough about football to realize that. I guarantee you if Randall were available, Beathard would bring him to San Diego in a heartbeat. But the bottom line is Randall is black, and some people don't want him to forget it. The NFL won't let him forget it.

There's also a theory out there that blacks don't have the mental capability to play quarterback. Once again, it was started by NFL owners and general managers who simply don't want blacks to be in any kind of leadership or decision-making position on their team. That applies to other positions, too. For a long time, there weren't any black middle linebackers in the NFL. For a long time, there weren't any black centers. And of course, there still aren't many black quarterbacks.

Those three positions are the key positions as far as decision making in football. The center has to make all the calls on the line, choose the blocking schemes and let everybody else know what to do. The middle linebacker makes all the calls on the defense, and the quarterback calls the offensive plays. It took a long time before blacks were allowed to play these positions because the owners didn't want to put a black in a position of authority. A lot of them still don't.

It's slowly changing in the league. Look at Mike Singletary. If it weren't for him, Chicago never would have had such a dominant defense. He makes all their calls. Last year San Diego started a black center, a rookie named Courtney Hall. And Dwight Stephens of the Miami Dolphins was probably the best center to play the game until he injured his knee. But if you look around the league, you really don't have a lot of black centers. And until we got the 34 Defense, with two middle linebackers, we didn't have a lot of black middle linebackers. Now you've usually got one black guy and one white guy at inside linebacker. Guess who normally makes the calls?

When it comes to quarterback, you're really talking about a leadership position. It's just like any other leadership position—general in the Army, an executive in Corporate America, or the President of the United States. We traditionally haven't had blacks in those positions. Some people will never accept blacks in those places.

What we're talking about is basic bigotry or racism, which we've still got throughout society. It has just rubbed off into the world of sports. Deep down inside, many of the NFL owners, general managers and coaches don't want a black quarterback, because they don't want a black man running their team.

If they can get away with it, they're going to overlook the young black quarterback coming out of college. They'll find some excuse for not drafting him or they'll move him to another position. The only time they're going to take a black quarterback is when he's obviously the best player available or their team is desperate to win. The Tampa

Bay Buccaneers drafted me in the first round in 1978 because they had just set an NFL record by losing their first twenty-six games and they wanted to win so badly they would have taken anyone. The other case is a Warren Moon or Randall Cunningham. They were just too good to be overlooked, although Moon had to go to Canada to prove himself before the NFL would touch him. But take my brother Mike, for example. Mike had a great career at Grambling, but the people in the NFL said he was too short. Mike is six feet tall and can play the game. What about Doug Flutie and Pat Haden? They aren't close to six feet, but the NFL couldn't wait to get them.

Once a black quarterback, or any black player for that matter, gets in the league, he has to deal with other kinds of discrimination. Look at the stories that came out during the Super Bowl concerning the league's drug-testing practices. What's ironic is Dexter Manley and I discussed that very subject early in the 1989 season. We talked about how it's almost always black players who are suspended for drug use. It doesn't affect me because I don't use drugs and I'm never in the company of players who do. But it's blatant racism to tip off the white players about drug tests and let the black players get caught.

Just look at what is happening. Virtually all of the players that have been suspended for drug use from the testing program have been black. Come on now. Drugs destroy black players, but they mess up many white players as well. In the NFL when things get messy, they also get murky and nobody really knows what is going on. That's no accident. That's typical of NFL management.

They also think blacks can't master the quarterback position. That's ludicrous. I've played eleven years of professional football and played for four different teams, and I've never been in a situation where I had trouble learning the offensive system. I've always been a team leader, too. One thing a black quarterback doesn't get is a chance to hang around. You either produce or you're gone. If you can't perform now, they don't want you.

The NFL generally doesn't want black quarterbacks as backups. That position is tailored for that young white quarterback who has all the promise. Not some young black guy who can't produce now, or an older black quarterback who has played in the league for some years.

They don't want you unless you can make a major contribution right now. They're not going to pay a black guy to be a backup. That's their mentality.

A lot of people say I'm the pioneer of black quarterbacks, but I don't want to take that credit. I believe people like James Harris and Joe Gilliam paved the way for me. They went through all the tough times and paid the high price. And they made it easier for me. I think I've made it easier today for the Moons, Cunninghams, Peetes and hopefully Andre Ware.

I've been fortunate to know James Harris since I was at Grambling. He's a very, very low-key individual. I know he went through some difficult times, but not once did he ever come to me and say, "Doug, these white people in this league don't think we can play." Not once did he ever say that, even though it is true. When I was around him, he was always a confidence builder.

Shack would tell me, "There's nobody out there who can throw the ball like you." He was trying to tell me to keep my head up no matter what happens and just get the job done. He never instilled in me that I wouldn't get a fair opportunity, and I appreciate that. I went in believing I could make it and that helped me overcome a lot of problems.

When I went to Tampa Bay in 1978, there was no doubt I was going to play, because they didn't really have anyone else. I was fortunate to have been drafted by the Buccaneers. I was at the right place at the right time. It was also good to play for a coach like John McKay, who didn't care if you were black, green, yellow or white. If you could get the job done, you could play for Coach McKay.

Other black guys haven't been so fortunate. Take Rodney Peete, for example. The Detroit Lions got him late in the draft, because the league put a rap on Rodney that he didn't have the arm to play in the NFL. It's amazing to me that they would say that. I don't think Joe Montana has a strong arm. But he's got great leadership and other abilities. There aren't that many quarterbacks in the league with great arms. You take away John Elway, Jim Everett and Jim Kelly, and there aren't many guys with strong arms. Nowadays Bernie Kosar can hardly throw it twenty yards. Do you think he would still be in the league if he was black?

Don't get me wrong, Bernie Kosar can play. But I'm not sure if a black quarterback was going through what Bernie is, that he would get the same break.

No question about it, the NFL overlooked Rodney's leadership abilities, because he's black. The guy went to a big-time school. He led Southern Cal every year. He knew how to win football games, so his leadership should have been a factor. But we are judged so differently as black quarterbacks. If you don't have the cannon, they're going to say you can't play in the NFL. If you can't drop back and throw a twenty-yard out on the line, which means it's going to travel about thirty-five yards, you can't play in this league. But if the white guy comes in and can barely get it there, they say he's got great touch. That's how they rate it.

Another thing they try to do is say a black guy can't pass the tests they give him. So they say he won't be able to learn the offense. Take for example Terrence Jones out of Tulane. He got drafted late by San Diego, and the Chargers wanted to make a wide receiver out of him, so he went to Canada. I talked to a couple scouts and they said the rap on Terrence was he couldn't pick it up. My goodness, I've been around some quarterbacks in this league who had trouble picking up some things, but you've got to give them a chance. But their mentality is they don't have time to spend on a black. They don't want to put in any time on a young black quarterback. You've got to be able to play right away, or they don't want you.

Somebody like Andre Ware has to play. He's the Heisman Trophy winner and you can't bury him. But look at Tony Rice and Major Harris. The NFL came up with excuses why they can't play quarterback in the league. Tony played in an offense at Notre Dame that didn't utilize his throwing ability. But they're not going to give him a chance to develop in the NFL. They're going to want to move Rice and Harris to some other position, and that's a shame.

Going from college football to the NFL is a big step. But it's just another adjustment you have to make. It's the same as going from high school to college. Some people in the league said I wasn't ready to play in the NFL because I went to a small black school, which didn't prepare me well enough to play pro ball. But if you check the history book, there are an awful lot of players out of black colleges who have made it big in the NFL. The all-time leading rusher, Walter Payton, just happens to be from Jackson State. At one time the all-time leading pass receiver was Charlie Joiner, who just happened to be from Grambling. And the guy who is on the road to breaking all the pass receiving records, Jerry Rice, is from Mississippi Valley State. They're all from those black colleges that supposedly don't prepare their players well enough to play in the NFL.

For anyone coming out of college, there are some adjustments you have to make to be able to play pro ball. There's no question about that. But it's an individual thing. It doesn't have anything to do with where you went to school or what color you are. It's just a matter of being able to pick up the terminology and offensive system of the team that gets you. Every team has different terminology, so you've got to start over whenever you go to a new team.

When I went to Tampa Bay, sure it was tough at first because I was coming right out of college. It's difficult for everybody. But if you study the offense hard enough for three or four weeks, with the coaches force feeding you, you're going to get the picture. You're going to be able to understand what the offense is all about. As the weeks go by, you're going to make more and more progress. Hopefully, your offensive line will give you time to read the defenses.

You've got to have some pass protection to be a successful quarterback. Remember the Oakland Raiders of old and how great they made Ken Stabler look. Stabler told me he could have played in a business suit, that's how much time he had to throw the football. What he meant was they had a great offensive line and he didn't have to read defenses. He could wait for somebody to get open. Besides that, he told me his best receiver, Cliff Branch, could outrun half the cars in the parking lot. So when you've got time and a great receiver, there's no way you can fail. How many quarterbacks today have time to stand in the pocket, look left, look right and come back and throw left? Not many. So that lets you know the Raiders of old were getting it done with Gene Upshaw and Art Shell and linemen like that. They were blowing people out.

Today, it's a different ballgame on the professional level. They've got so many different schemes, you never know what the defense is going to throw at you. They try to change it up all the time and disguise their coverages. One time you might think you see the cornerback roll up, and all of a sudden he rolls up and then runs off. It's a thinking man's game. As a quarterback, you've got to be thinking from the time you walk up to the line of scrimmage, to the time you're calling the cadence, to your first step. You're thinking on the run, so it's a tough job. When they first get up there, a lot of young quarterbacks have problems because they're thinking so much that they never relax and get into the game.

Once you get a feel for what's going on, you begin to relax and start understanding things. I don't think you ever pick it all up. I think every day, every year, you're still learning, because things are always changing. Somebody is always coming up with some new way to stop you. You've got coaches spending hours on the blackboard figuring out ways to disguise different defenses and how to get things done. So you never pick it all up. Anytime you think you've got it all figured out, somebody throws something new at you.

A few years ago, the Chicago Bears went on to win the Super Bowl because they came out with the 46 Defense. Everybody had almost mastered the 34 and the 4-3 and the Flex and the Unders and the Overs. And all of a sudden, Chicago came up with the 46 Defense and the Solid Dubs. So they were throwing something new at you, and you had to go back to the drawing board. The 46 Defense has three linemen in the middle, a wide end to the one side and two linebackers to the other side. Then the Solid Dubs Fist is the safety, who comes up in the hole. He can blitz or drop back in coverage. You never know what he's going to do, so that puts a lot of pressure on the offense. You can only do so much. You always have to be ready to throw a blitz breakoff. But you've got to know what to do if they're not blitzing. It's a tough defense to prepare for.

Now the Rams have come up with a new defense using two down linemen and five linebackers. So you never know what people are going to try defensively. You've always got to be studying the game and be prepared to make adjustments.

I've been fortunate to play for Joe Gibbs at Washington. Believe me, I learned more football in my first year at Washington than I learned in five years at Tampa Bay. The Redskins have the schemes and know what they want to do. They've got a clue. Whereas, in Tampa, there weren't that many clues. I can remember at Tampa when I went back to pass, I had the responsibility of picking up both safeties. If they came after me, it was my responsibility to get rid of the football. In Washington, they spend a lot more time on protecting the quarterback and giving the quarterback specific reads and saying, "This is what you do if this happens." But no matter what play the Redskins end up using, whether they run the ball or throw it, they want to make sure the quarterback doesn't get hit. That's why it's a great system. They pick up the defenses. And Coach Gibbs spends an awful lot of time coming up with schemes to do that.

Professional football is a business. It's your livelihood, so you've got to know what's going on all the time. You've got to put in the hours reviewing your own plays and studying the defenses. In college, you can get away with relying on your athletic ability. We had a lot of great athletes at Grambling. I played my first two years, because I had the ability to drop back and throw the football. Plus, I was fortunate enough to have a great offensive line, receivers like Sammy White and Dwight Scales and pretty good running backs. I really started learning when I was a junior and we had lost guys like Sammy and Dwight. That's when you have to grow up and take control. As a quarterback, you have to find out what's going on.

By my senior year, Coach Eddie Robinson didn't have to send in the plays anymore. I called my own plays, because I knew how he thought, I knew the system we were using, and I knew we ran things in series. If we got into the 28 series, we had certain things that we ran: wing back around, wing back counter, the 28 pass, the 28 reverse, the screen. Once we got into a series, I stayed with it, because I knew that's what Coach Rob would have done. I liked him having confidence in me. I wanted him to be able to depend on me. But it took two years for me to get to that point.

My last two years, when we had the ball, it was my team—Coach Rob didn't have to worry about the offense. We led the nation in scoring my senior year, averaging forty-two points a game. So there wasn't that much Coach Rob had to do, other than make sure we practiced all week, make sure everyone was healthy and then put us on the ball field. We had this trainer named Dan, and whenever we'd get on the bus for a game, he used to say, "Is Doug here?" They'd say yeah, and he'd say, "Well, let's go."

Even though Coach Rob did a great job getting me ready, professional football is much different than college ball. In college, I don't think the guys realize how important it is to get totally involved in what you're doing. Once you become a pro, that's your job and you treat it differently.

Lately, the game has become so complex. You've got the advent of computers and at the same time the athletes have become so much better. When I first went to Tampa Bay, I didn't have a fear in the world of a linebacker. I thought I was stronger than the average linebacker. I could run over the average linebacker or I could run past the average linebacker. I even ran over some defensive linemen.

Today, I wouldn't even attempt some of those things. When you've got people like Lawrence Taylor at 240 pounds, you can't do that. You can't run over linebackers like Carl Banks, Cornelius Bennett, Rickey Jackson and Pat Schwilling. They run 4.5 forties and are as strong as linemen. You'd better keep your butt in the pocket or you'll get killed.

Randall Cunningham and John Elway are two of the few quarterbacks who even have a chance to outrun a linebacker today. There aren't many others who can do it. That's why protecting the quarterback is so important. In the past, linebackers didn't blitz or weren't getting to the quarterback as much. Now those linebackers are coming at full speed and they've got open shots at you. That's why you've got so many injuries. I think that's the biggest change in the last ten years. You used to have a lot of guys who stayed in the league a long time, but that doesn't happen much any more. You've got to be an exceptional football player to stay a long time in the league today.

With so many fast linebackers, you must have a good offensive scheme or you don't have a chance to keep those guys off you. Everything is a quick decision now. Look at San Francisco's offense, everything is a quick read. If you watch Montana, as soon as he leaves the center, he's ready to throw the football. One, two, three, he's going to get it to somebody. If Rice isn't coming in, he'll get it off to Roger Craig. If Craig isn't there, he'll get it to the tight end. If he's not there, let's get it to the fullback. That's how their offense works. You have to play that way in today's game. It's no longer a game of get yourself a full drop and wait in the pocket until somebody comes open. You don't have that kind of time anymore.

Even if you're going to take a full seven-step drop, you must have an idea of what you're going to do with the ball. You're reading on the run. Once you take those first three steps and you find out where that safety is going, your mind has to be focused on where you're going to throw the ball. It's no longer the Stabler theory, where you hit the seventh step and start looking around. Now when you hit seven, you're planting and throwing.

I was able to play in the league so long because I'm durable and adaptable. I don't think there's a quarterback that has been in this league, besides Jim Plunkett, Lynn Dickey, Archie Manning and Phil Simms, who has taken the physical abuse that I have and still survived. I think my durability played a big part in why I lasted so long in the NFL. I've had knee surgery five times, a back operation, an emergency appendectomy, a broken jaw, a separated shoulder and a bunch of less serious injuries. To play in this league, you've got to be able to deal with pain. Lots of it.

Also, I'm nobody's dummy. I may not be a Phi Beta Kappa, but if you put me in a situation, I'm going to have an idea of what we've got to do to move the football or get points.

I don't think anyone goes in and masters the game. I think you can only go in and play within the limits of your game plan. The Redskins probably have as complex an offense as there is in the NFL. When we walked in that meeting room on Wednesdays to get the game plan, the blood pressure in your head immediately went up. You saw all of these new plays on the board and you knew you had only two days to get it down and worry about what you were going to do on Sunday. You had your first-down situations, your second downs and your third downs. It was all up there on the board. In the Redskins' system, the main thing you've got to do is learn the formation and then worry about what you're going to run out of that formation. The plays don't change that much, but the formations are going to be different every week. As the quarterback, you've got to get everyone in the right formation before you run a play.

I think I've shown I can pick up any offense. I've played for Tampa Bay, two USFL teams and Washington, and I've always been able to pick up the offense well enough to perform. That's the bottom line. You've got to be ready to perform. It's even tougher when you're playing backup, because it's easy to get lackadaisical if you're not playing. But you must always remember you're just one play away from playing. All it takes is one injury and you've got to take over.

The 1987 season was probably my greatest year as far as being ready to play. When things didn't go right for Jay Schroeder, I came off the bench ready to lead the team, and I know Coach Gibbs liked that. That's why he likes to have a veteran as a backup. He knows a veteran has the mental capability and maturity to be ready to play when given the opportunity. I was prepared to play just like I would have been if I had started. As a result, I performed well, and we were able to go to the Super Bowl.

I've never had to pull my hair out worrying about an offensive scheme or game plan. I've always been able to pick it up and work within the system. But I was fortunate to get the opportunity to prove myself. Most black quarterbacks don't ever get that chance.

I remember James Harris told me about his experiences being recruited by some of the big colleges. One of the coaches that wanted him was Duffy Daugherty at Michigan State. When Shack made his visit to Michigan State, they had him out throwing the football. Duffy Daugherty looked at him and said, "Boy, you've got a good arm. But you've got great hands." Shack said he knew right then he wasn't going to Michigan State. If he wanted to play quarterback, he had to go to a small school, so he went to Grambling. I grew up fifteen miles from LSU, but they never even talked to me about playing there. They still don't play black quarterbacks at LSU.

In order for blacks to get a fair shot at playing quarterback in the NFL, it has to start at the college level. We've got to have some more Andre Wares. We've got to have a black quarterback at Miami. We've got to have a black quarterback at LSU. We've got to have a black quarterback at Stanford and Illinois. The reason I mention these schools is because they're the ones throwing the football. Until these situations occur, we're always going to have a lack of black quarterbacks in the NFL. Most of them are now being used as athletes. Run first, and pass second. They're not given a chance to pick up all the things they need to pick up to become a passing quarterback in the NFL.

It even starts earlier than that. There are some high schools that have problems with using a black quarterback. We've even got some peewee teams that have trouble letting a black kid play quarterback. I've got a little nephew who played peewee football, and he could throw the ball much better than the guy who was playing quarterback. But the quarterback had to be white.

Once black kids get a chance to play quarterback in peewee leagues, high school and college, it will be up to the NFL owners, general managers and coaches to give them a chance. They've got to stop finding excuses for not drafting black quarterbacks or trying to move them to new positions. They've got to open the door to black quarterbacks.

You've got to be given the opportunity. I got my chance, and I did something with it. I think the proof is in the pudding.

I think Warren Moon has proved he can play with anybody; he's been in two straight Pro Bowls. I think Randall Cunningham has proved it. I think Rodney Peete has proved it. Rodney can really play. But if they had not been given a shot, they never could have done it.

To me, it's sad that it had to take a Super Bowl for some people to think a black quarterback could play in the NFL. I personally hate the idea that my going to the Super Bowl shattered the myth that blacks can't play quarterback. How did I get to the Super Bowl? They didn't say, "Here, Doug Williams, you play in the Super Bowl and show us if you can play." It wasn't like that.

I didn't get a chance to quarterback the Redskins because I could not play. Moon didn't get $2 million because he could not play. They didn't give Randall $3 million because he could not play. So somebody thinks enough of these guys to let them play. Black quarterbacks are just as capable as white quarterbacks, and I don't think it took a Super Bowl to prove that.

4

Men at War

I've never put together an all-defensive team in my mind. But I've thought a lot about some players on defense who can easily strike fear in your heart.

As far as I'm concerned, everything starts up front. The linemen and linebackers determine what kind of defense you have. The defensive lineman who stands out the most is Reggie White. Reggie is the ultimate lineman. He combines strength, speed, agility and intelligence. When you play Philadelphia, Reggie is going to find a way to beat you.

Richard Dent of Chicago is going to beat you with his speed around the corners. He's going to get there. Richard is also stronger than you think he is. Coming off the right end, he has one of the best left-arm moves in the game. He lifts that tackle up and gets to the quarterback. If you've got a quarterback who doesn't step up in the pocket, he's going to be in trouble with Richard, because he's coming up the field at you.

Going back a few years, Al "Bubba" Baker was the best. In my first few years in the league, Detroit had the most consistent defensive lines in football, and Bubba was at the top of his game. You're talking about a guy who's 6-7 or 6-8 and comes flying around that corner right at you.

I thought Alan Page was quick off the tackle until I played against Keith Millard for the first time. It's amazing how quick Keith is. I've only seen one offensive lineman neutralize Millard, and that was Raleigh McKenzie of the Redskins. When we played the Vikings in the 1987 NFL championship game, Millard did not get to me all day. But I don't know if anyone else has ever stopped Millard.

At inside linebacker you've got Mike Singletary, who's the best to ever play that position. Bar none, he's the greatest at middle linebacker. He knows the position, he runs the whole Chicago defense, and he will butt heads with anybody. Anybody.

But the greatest player is Lawrence Taylor. He's the greatest to ever play the game of football. It's a pleasure watching Lawrence play football, whether he's playing against you or against somebody else. You can't help but admire what he does. You almost become a cheerleader. You just want to sit there and watch for what he'll do next.

I like the way Lawrence plays football because he's going to make something happen. He's either going to make the tackle or make you fumble every time. Stripping the football from players is one of his specialties. Last year when the Redskins opened against the Giants, Gerald Riggs fumbled the football, and it was Lawrence Taylor who caused it. He ran all the way around from his right side, came across the field, chased Riggs down on the sidelines and raked the ball.

We all know Lawrence has had some problems. I often wonder if he didn't have those problems, would we have to outlaw him from football? An amazing player, he gives you 110 percent on every play. Until you've sat on the sidelines, you can't appreciate what he does. A lot of people say they don't use him on pass coverage. Why should they? If he can get to the quarterback, there's not going to be a pass to cover. When you prepare for the Giants, you have to prepare for Lawrence.

The secondary is hard to pick. There are an awful lot of good defensive backs. But I believe the defensive front dictates how good the defensive backs are. As an overall secondary, I would have to rate the San Francisco 49ers as having the best. They've got Ronnie Lott and Jeff Fuller at the safeties, and they've had several good cornerbacks, including Eric Wright. When we played them in 1988, they had the most balanced secondary I've ever faced. They could play man-on-man. They could play zone. They could play whatever they wanted to play, and they played it well.

As far as the toughest overall defense, there have been some great ones in the last twelve years. Early in my career, I had to play against the Los Angeles Rams when they had Jack Youngblood and Fred Dryer at the ends. They weren't overpowering, but they were intelligent and knew where to be at the right time.

I think the Chicago Bears have always had great defenses. In the late 1970s and early 1980s, they didn't have that dominating defense yet, but they were always physical. They wanted to make you pay for everything you got. Back then, Doug Plank was their intimidator. He would come up and hit you as hard as he could. Then he'd stand over you and ask, "Are you all right?"

The dominating defenses in the NFL started to develop in the early to mid-1980s. I think by far the most intimidating team was the Bears. When Buddy Ryan brought in that 46 defense, it changed everything. It has to be the most dominating scheme that I've ever seen. Not that every player was dominating, but they had the people in the right position to make it a dominating defense.

The Bears' defense all started with Mike Singletary. He's just such a great athlete at that position. Then they had Otis Wilson, who was another outstanding athlete who could run and make a lot of things happen. There was also Dan Hampton—bigger than life and a tough, tough man. Dan was always a force. It really helped them when they added Richard Dent to rush the passer from the end position. And Steve McMichael was a constant performer.

It didn't really matter who they had in the secondary, because their front seven was so strong. Dave Duerson played a monster of a safety, but with the Bears' front so dominating, you didn't really care who was playing in the secondary. That was exploited this past year when they couldn't get the type of pass rush they once did. Teams were able to throw the football on their secondary.

Buddy Ryan was obviously important to the Bears. I don't know if he's the best defensive mind in the game, but he's probably one of the most liked coaches and can come up with some of the best schemes to put you in an awful situation. I can remember when I was playing

against him at Tampa Bay. He was either going to make you look bad
or he was going to look bad. They were either going to make a big play
on defense or you were going to make a big play on offense. He was
willing to take that gamble. They played a lot of man-on-man. I can remember one game in Tampa when Jimmy Giles caught two passes
against them for over 160 yards, because they were gambling and we
caught them.

I think the biggest thing that the Bears miss is Buddy's personality. Buddy is a guy who believes in his players. Everybody I know who
played for Buddy liked him. Whereas, Mike Ditka has a different personality. I don't think Mike cares about anybody. Maybe that's just
what's on the outside. I think deep down inside, Mike has to have
some compassion for somebody. But if you just watch him on the
sidelines, you think he doesn't give a darn about anyone on the team.
Buddy isn't that way at all. He's a compassionate coach. He cared
about Mike Singletary. He was interested in Dan Hampton and Otis
Wilson. You've got to love those guys. When you show those guys
that you care about them, they're going to give you everything
they've got. I think that's what happened to the Bears when Buddy
left.

The Philadelphia Eagles aren't far away from the great Bears defenses. They have the best defensive front in football since the Pittsburgh Steelers had the "Steel Curtain." The Eagles have a lot of guys
on that defensive front who are underrated. Everybody knows about
Reggie White. But Jerome Brown and Clyde Simmons can play. I think
what Buddy needs is a Singletary-like middle linebacker. He also
needs another athletic linebacker on the weak side and a player or two
in the secondary.

But when those guys up front are playing, they're the best in the
business. Any quarterback who plays against the Eagles is going to
take punishment. You're going to pay. Their style is to intimidate you.
If you're a quarterback with a very small heart, you might as well go
on to the house.

Buddy's defenses cause a lot of fear. I think back to the Super
Bowl when the Bears played New England. The worst thing I've ever
seen in my life was when Tony Eason folded up against the Bears rush
and they were still six yards away from him. That's no heart. That's
the kind of intimidation Buddy likes his team to give out. That's what

the Eagles are doing now. If you don't have the determination to stay in that pocket and pay the price to get the football down field, you're in trouble.

I've played against the Eagles the last four years, and they've never beat me. I think it's a matter of determination. I could have gone down. I could have accepted the fact that they were tearing my ass up. But my attitude is if it's going to be a dogfight, we're all going to fight. I think the Eagles respect me. I think they realize if you're going to beat Doug Williams, you're going to have to keep knocking him down and hope that something happens to him. They realize they're not going to take away my heart. They never have. But I've seen them take the heart out of a lot of quarterbacks.

How do you handle the great defensive players? You don't. What you have to do is focus your offense away from their strength. You try to find out things they don't do well. I think the prime example is Lawrence Taylor. What you don't want to do is run away from Lawrence, because he's going to chase you down. He doesn't really have a weakness per se, but it's obvious his strength is to run down people. So you try to go at him and get him fighting off linemen, instead of just running around them.

When you're making your game plan against the Giants, you want to run at Lawrence Taylor to cut down on his pursuit. If you're going to throw on the Giants, you want to make sure he's not being blocked one-on-one. You have to put somebody else out there, so that he has to go around or through two people. That's the only way you'll have time to throw the football. You have to go through a lot of preparation to get ready to play against a dominating player like him. You have to find a way to neutralize him and give yourself the opportunity to do some things. Yet, you have to realize with a guy like Lawrence you're not going to keep him out of the ballgame all day.

Philadelphia really does a good job of utilizing Reggie White's ability. They might line him up on the end. They might line him up at tackle, or they can put him at nose. They try to throw you off balance by moving him around. Buddy Ryan knows every team is going to try to find a way to keep Reggie out of the backfield. But what Philly has in its favor are the guys like Brown and Simmons who can play. They're almost as tough as Reggie. I think Jerome Brown should have gone to the Pro Bowl. He's one of the best tackles in the game. But what really helps Jerome is that he gets into a one-on-one situation most of the time, because they have to double up on Reggie.

One thing that a quarterback can do to slow down players like Reggie, Lawrence and Jerome is to stagger the count every now and then. It prevents them from getting a good jump on you by throwing off their timing. If you can keep them from getting into a rhythm, you might be able to keep them off you for awhile.

The most important thing for a quarterback is to have a quick release. When the defensive linemen can't get to the quarterback, it frustrates them. They live for getting to the quarterback. That's their whole game. You have to be able to get rid of the ball before they get there. That really tees them off. They've been working so darn hard all day to get that sack, and all of a sudden, you let the ball go. That drives them crazy. Sooner or later, they start to let up and think, "Man, I'm not going to get there." That's what the quarterback has to be able to do.

While the quarterback is trying to stay away from certain players, he's also trying to find the guy that he can attack. You throw at the defensive back who has trouble covering. You run at the defensive lineman who doesn't play the run well, and you go at the linebacker who plays soft. That's what you build your game plan around. When we played the Dallas Cowboys, we would stay away from Everson Walls and go right at Ron Francis. But if you go at them too much, you end up making them pretty good players.

The key aspect of reading a defense is having time to do it. So to me, the ability to read defenses boils down to a good offensive line. They have to do it for you.

Since I've been in the league, it's always been assumed that the safety tips you off as to what is happening. They give you a good indication if it's going to be zone, man or blitz. It it's a blitz, the safety is usually playing a little closer than normal. When it's a zone, they're going to be a little deeper and the corners are going to play outside on you. Nine times out of ten, when it's man, the corner is going to be head-up with the receiver, and the safety is going to be a little closer. Most of the time when they're playing man, the linebackers are blitzing and one of the safeties has to pick up the running back coming out of the backfield. That's why he has to be in closer.

But the real challenge for the quarterback is being able to anticipate when the defense is disguising. The good teams are very good at disguising coverages, and that gives the offense trouble. The Redskins do a lot of movement and formation changes, which gives the quarterback a chance to figure out what the defense is doing. Eventually, they've got to declare what defense they're going to play. You usually know from the snap of the ball if the defense is going to play zone or man on you.

In recent years, the game has become so computerized and complex. It's really complicated with the Redskins. Joe Gibbs doesn't believe in a lot of audibles. What he relies on is checkoffs. If the other team is in a certain defense, you do this. If they do something else, you do that.

You have to decide what kind of game plan you want, whether it's a running game or pass-oriented. The Redskins usually want to be able to control the ball with the run. That's what most teams try to do. If you can move the ball on the ground, that's going to set up your passing.

A typical first-down play for the Redskins would be an off-tackle run or a sweep. We called it a flat or outside run. Against a team like the New York Giants, for example, my call in the huddle would be "Check with me flat" or "Check with me outside." What that means is I'm going to the line, look over the defense and then decide where we're going to run the ball.

When we played the Giants, the first thing I'd look for is where they've got Lawrence Taylor lined up.

If Lawrence was lined up on the right side of the defense, we'd have to go with a running play to our left. So I would go to the line and call "Green 33, Green 33." The odd numbers are to your left and the even numbers are to your right. The 33 run is off tackle. If you wanted to go outside, you would call 37.

However, you can always go with a pass if you catch the defense in a press technique. That means they're going to play bump-and-run and they're in a man-to-man coverage. Usually, the cornerbacks will walk up and play slightly inside the wide receivers when they're going to play bump-and-run. The Redskins always liked to get into a man-to-man situation because we had the receivers to beat that coverage.

In that event, I might call "Brown 12" to check off to a pass to one of our receivers. That audible is for a pass called Charlie Hitch, which gives the receiver the option of breaking away from the defensive back. It's been one of the most effective plays for the Redskins.

On second down, you're probably going to go with a pass, depending on how many yards you need and the defense you're playing against. If it's a team like the Eagles, you're definitely going to have to throw on second down if you need four or more yards.

With the Eagles' overpowering defensive line, you have to throw some kind of quick pass or they'll put you in a bind. You must take a quick five-step drop and get rid of the ball. That's all the time you'll have before Reggie White and friends are going to be on you. All you can really do is hope to gain about five yards and get into a third-and-short situation.

The first thing you look for against the Eagles is where Reggie is lined up. You always want to know where he's coming from. Then you look at their cornerbacks. If they're head up with the receivers, they're probably in man-to-man. If they're back a few yards and looking at the quarterback, it's probably a zone. Since the Eagles have a four-man front, they've only got three linebackers to drop into a zone. So that means they'll have bigger holes in their zone.

A typical second-down call against the Eagles would be 333. That's a pass play where the outside receiver runs a twelve-yard out, the inside guy goes twelve yards and hooks into the zone, and the backs run a flare. Most of the time, you're going to have to find the tight end or H-back over the middle.

You might be able to pick on the Eagles' young cornerback, Eric Allen. But that's not something you can count on because they'll try to give him help. Their free safety, Wes Hawkins, will roll to his side and help him over there. So you really can't look just to one spot.

On third and long, you're going to see a zone nine times out of ten. But against a team like the Chicago Bears, you can expect some heat. You know they're going to come after you. A conservative team like the New Orleans Saints will sit back in a zone. But the Bears rely on pressuring the quarterback. They believe if you hit the quarterback enough, he's going to make a mistake eventually. They'll send an outside linebacker after the quarterback and make him pay. When the Bears used to have Wilbur Marshall and Richard Dent on the same side, they were devastating. Now they've got a bunch of young guys at outside linebacker and they haven't established themselves yet.

That's why they had so much trouble against the pass last season. They had probably the worst pass defense in the league.

When it's third down, you know you must get the ball down field. In that situation, the two most effective routes are a deep square or a deep curl. However, if the safety makes a mistake, there's a chance you can hit a receiver going deep on a post.

Most defenses are going to make you catch the ball in front of them. They're going to hit the receiver hard and make him pay for catching the ball. There's also a chance there will be a bad throw and the defense can come up with an interception.

In my years with the Redskins, we had quite a bit of success in third and long, because we had three outstanding receivers. Art Monk made some catches that would turn your head. Gary Clark would make some incredible one-handed catches. Sometimes Gary would drop the ball, because he was trying to run with it too soon. But he usually made up for it. And Ricky Sanders could do a lot with the ball after he caught it. He's a former running back from Southwest Texas State.

On third and short, it didn't matter who the Redskins were playing, the ball was probably going to Kelvin Bryant. K.B. is the best third-down back in the NFL. Defenses had a tough time trying to find a way to stop him from catching the ball on third down. We could always count on him.

I think Coach Gibbs has one of the best game plans in the league. He studies the other team completely. He puts in his game plan based on what the other team has done in the past, and he sticks to it. He always gives the quarterback the green light to audible to a certain pass. But there's very few changes made out on the field. Almost everything is planned beforehand. You play within the limits.

I understand that the New York Jets new coaching staff thinks Ken O'Brien is holding the ball too long, because he was reading the defense. So they're going to get rid of the reading system and go to a progressive system, which is what the 49ers have done since Joe Montana has been there. It's a progress: if the tight end is open, hit him; if he's covered, hit the wide receiver; and if he's covered, hit the running back. Whereas, if you're reading, you're studying the safety and thinking, "Ok, if you're going to play zone, the safety is going to fade to the right, so get away from him and throw it left." It all depends on the system you're playing in. The Redskins use a reading system. We wanted the safety to dictate to us what the coverage was and where to go with the football.

Reading defenses can be effective only if you have time to read. The disadvantage is it gives the defense a chance to get to you. If the blocking isn't good, you don't have a chance to read. When I was in Tampa, some people tried to say I couldn't read defenses. But the truth was I never had time to read. There isn't a quarterback alive who can read defenses and throw the football before he gets set.

The 49ers are one of the few teams that have been successful with the progressive system. The reason is they've got the personnel to make it work. If you get the ball to Tom Rathman, he picks up twelve yards. If you get it to Roger Craig, he might break it. If you get it to Jerry Rice, who knows what might happen. And if you don't feel like throwing it to those guys, just turn around and throw it to John Taylor on the post. The 49ers know what capabilities they have in their players, and they use them the right way. Joe Montana comes out from the center ready to throw the football. And it's awfully hard to stop him.

For quarterbacks some things are taught and some are caught. As far as knowing when to scramble, I think it's all instinct. A lot of quarterbacks leave the pocket too soon. Those are the ones with scared feet.

I always thought the safest place for a quarterback is in the pocket. At least you've got some protection there. Once you get outside, there's no help. It's you against the world. Of course, some quarterbacks make things happen. Randall Cunningham can do it. He's an athlete. Steve Young is an athlete. John Elway is an athlete. But most quarterbacks are not able to scramble like those guys can. I think having good feet is important. Sometimes, that's better than being a scrambler. If you can move up, move to the right and left, and know when to step back, that makes the difference. That isn't something you learn. You have to have a sixth sense for it.

I hate it when a quarterback coach makes you practice scrambling. It really irks me to see a quarterback practice that. First of all, I don't want a quarterback who's going to scramble. You only scramble when you have to. And that's not something you can teach. It's just like speed. You can't teach it and you can't catch it. You either have it or you don't.

In my opinion, a right-handed quarterback should never get

sacked by a defensive end coming around the tackle on the right side. It just should not happen. If you can see the guy coming around at you, you should be able to do something about it. I can understand getting blindsided every once in a while, but you've got to be able to feel that and step up. Getting hit from the right side is inexcusable.

There are a few tricks that quarterbacks learn through the years. One of them is moving your foot before the snap. I've gotten away with a foot movement every now and then. Those defensive linemen are biting at the bit to get to the quarterback, and they're watching his foot for the first movement. Alan Page was the best at that. His eyes would be glued on to your foot. You couldn't even think about having a false step, because he had you. I've been in games where he almost handed the football off for me. Once your foot moved, he was gone.

I learned to put my weight on the heel of my foot. Then when I'd raise it up a little, sometimes they'd come early. But you can't do that too many times. Really, there aren't that many tricks you can learn. It's a team effort, it's a team game, and everything works within the framework of the team.

I've been fortunate to have played with some great receivers, especially at Washington. I think it's up to the quarterback to know his receivers. Once you've worked with a guy, you should know what he can do, what he can't do and what he should do. The quarterback has to be able to judge for himself if the receiver is going to get open. His speed, his height, or whatever shouldn't make a difference. You should be able to throw the ball to him.

A few years ago, there was a lot of talk at LSU that Tommy Hodson only had short receivers to throw to after Wendell Davis left to go to the Bears. That should never have been a factor. The quarterback has the ball in his hands, and he should be able to control everything. So what if you have short receivers. Nolan Ryan doesn't pitch to the same size guy every time. He brings it up or down. The quarterback has to adjust the same way. When I was at Grambling, my receiver was Robert Woods who was five-feet-seven. I adjusted and just threw the ball a little lower.

A quarterback has to be in charge of the offense in every way. In the huddle, you might have a couple linemen talking about what's going on up front. But as a quarterback, it's your huddle. Nobody is supposed to be talking except you. The quarterback's first priority is to get the respect of his teammates and establish that this is his house and he's going to do the talking.

I've been fortunate to play with guys who gave me that respect. They recognized that Doug is going to call the shots. Everyone else keeps quiet. That's when you realize you have the respect of the other players.

After calling the play, the quarterback might share something that he's seen. He might tell the linemen to be alert for the blitz or watch the backside. He could tell the receiver to look for the fade if they play bump and run, or he might say to look for the post if the safety doesn't get deep. Just little reminders like that.

To run the offense, you have to be a leader. Everyone has to believe in the quarterback. A rah-rah guy is not going to make it in the NFL. You have to lead by example. What I mean by that is not throwing TDs, but getting off the ground when they knock you on your ass. You get up, dust yourself off and then pat your lineman on the back and say, "Get it next time." That's the type of thing that earns respect. In the Super Bowl, when I got off that ground and limped back out there in pain, that created respect from my teammates.

Football is a man's game. It's contact. You've got to show the other guy that you're tougher than he is. You can't lay on the ground or come out of the game. You've got to get up and go right back at them. Not only do you get the respect of your teammates, the defense comes to respect you. The reason I've been successful against Philly is they know I'm not going to quit. They know they're going to have to keep coming after me, because I'm not going anywhere.

In certain situations, a quarterback has to be an innovator. He has to be able to ad-lib. There are times when he has to take it upon himself to make things happen. Not all the time, because that's what the team is all about. But there are times when you have to deviate from what you're supposed to do and come up with something creative. Of course, you're going to be wrong sometimes and you're going to get chewed out by the coach. Other times, you're going to do some good things, and the coach isn't going to do anything but smile at you.

I think most coaches like a quarterback who is daring, who is cocky and who can walk to the sidelines and say, "The heck with that play.'' They respect that. They understand that if you don't want to run a certain play, then you must have an idea of what's happening. You know what to run.

Coaches respect that type of quarterback. People talk about Terry Bradshaw having a bad relationship with Chuck Noll. Well, Chuck didn't care about that. Who worries about a relationship when you've got a competitor like Bradshaw? Chuck just wanted him to go out and kick some behinds. Bradshaw was a competitor. I'm sure he did a lot of things he wasn't supposed to do. But he's got four Super Bowl rings to make up for it.

You show me a quarterback who doesn't have some cockiness, who doesn't ad-lib some of the time, and I'll show you a quarterback who doesn't win. I've always been willing to take chances. I've also come to the sidelines angry about some plays that were called and I've told the coach how I felt about it. They accept that, because they know I'm just competing to the best of my ability. They know I'm going to give them everything I've got. And that's the bottom line for a quarterback.

A coach wants a quarterback whose mind is set on winning. That's what it's all about. That's why Coach Gibbs brought me to the Redskins in the first place. Coach Gibbs is all about winning, and he knows I'm a winner. Even though I wasn't healthy the last couple of years, I still instilled confidence in the Redskins and I still provided leadership. Not only that, but people in the NFL realize that for me to have accomplished what I've done, I had to be tough. You've got to be tough to play quarterback in this league. If you don't have a lot of heart, this isn't the business for you.

5

Bo, Joe and Jerry

Some of the most friendly, easy-going guys I know are offensive linemen and wide receivers. On the offensive side, you've got a different
type of individual. They're more conservative, easier to get along
with, and generally nicer people. When I think of a typical offensive
player, I think of Ricky Sanders. He's always got a big grin on his face.
Gary Clark is the same way. They're just very content, happy guys,
and that's generally what you'll find on offense. It's totally different
from defense, where the guys are brought up to tear off heads.

Offensive players can't afford to be overly aggressive. You have to
be somewhat tentative, because you've got to be thinking and planning ahead. An offensive lineman just can't go after somebody and try
to knock him into the ground. He's got to be concentrating on his assignment. He's got to get great position, have his hands on the pads,
and keep his man where he wants him. The only exception is when
you're pulling on a run. Then an offensive lineman can be reckless and
hit anything that moves. But that's the exception. Defensive players
have to get to the ball any way they can. That means they have to get
around somebody or run over them. Defense is a physical game, and
offense is a thinking game.

Of course, the quarterback has to do more thinking than anyone else on offense. He's got to be aware of everything going on, and he's got to take charge. The best quarterback in the game is Joe Montana. Joe is a fighter. Joe is a great competitor. Most of all, Joe knows how to win.

I think Jim McMahon is a winner, too. I really like Jim, even though I might be in a minority. He doesn't really have great ability and never did. But he's always had tremendous leadership skills. Jim is a leader, and that's more important than ability. I also respect Jim for his cockiness. He basically told the Bears organization to kiss off, and yet they continued to play him for a long time. That shows how valuable he was to the team. And look where they've gone without him.

Dan Marino is a player I really admire because he's willing to take chances. In that regard, he's a lot like Terry Bradshaw. They're daring quarterbacks. Dan has played with some good receivers, and he's made them look great.

I think Warren Moon probably has the best release in the game. He has such a good, high over-head release. And Warren is really a tough guy. If you knock him down, you know he's going to get right back up and come back after you.

Without a doubt, the most entertaining quarterback in the NFL is Randall Cunningham. Sometimes I can't believe what he does out on the field. His ability to escape from a jam is unbelievable. No matter who is coming after him, he always seems to get away. And once he's in the open, nobody is going to catch him. I just love to watch Randall play.

What may surprise some people is that I really like Phil Simms. Phil really reminds me of myself, because he's had to overcome so many injuries. He was there in New York when the Giants were just starting to build a team. He took a lot of pounding, but he stuck it out and led the Giants to the Super Bowl. I admire him for that.

Going back a few years the quarterback who really stands out is Archie Manning. I really have to take my hat off to him. Archie was a great competitor on a team that was never very good. Another guy just like Archie is Jim Plunkett. Everyone thought he was dead at New England. Then he went out to California and was revived. He had some great years with the Raiders.

I think the toughest quarterback that I've ever seen is Lynn

Dickey. When Lynn played for Green Bay, he was always getting beat up. He had to have a rod placed in his leg, but he kept playing and sacrificing himself for the team.

The quarterback with the best timing and anticipation was Dan Fouts. Dan knew where his receivers were going to be all the time. That's what made the Chargers' passing game so effective. He had a sixth sense that enabled him to anticipate exactly where the receiver was going to run and he had the arm to get it there.

Of course, I couldn't mention quarterbacks without including Terry Bradshaw. More than anything else, Terry was a winner. Some people liked to say he was dumb. If that's true, there are a lot of quarterbacks out there who would like to be that dumb. Terry was one of the greatest to ever play the game. He knew how to fight people off, and he had a gun for an arm.

I also admire Joe Namath and Kenny Stabler. Joe guaranteed a win against a great Colts team and he pulled it off. What more do you need to say about Namath? He deserves to be right up there with the best. Stabler was fortunate to have played with the Raiders when they were supremely talented. They had a tremendous football team. But Snake was a super leader. He also had a lot of fun off the field, and I think it's important that you enjoy your career because it doesn't last forever.

The Redskins have two promising young quarterbacks in Mark Rypien and Stan Humphries. I've always liked Ryp. He isn't a thing like Jay Schroeder. Ryp doesn't have that big ego. He's just a hard-working guy who's easy to get along with.

I think Ryp's future will depend a lot on what happens to the people around him. The Redskins have plenty of talent on the team right now. But you never know what might happen down the road. Ryp is a smart quarterback. He's one of the sharpest guys I know. And he's in the right system. Joe Gibbs will turn him into a good quarterback.

Stan has a lot of potential, too. But his future will boil down to getting a chance to play. Coach Gibbs isn't going to play two quarterbacks. Stan has a great deal of natural ability, really much more than Ryp, but there's more to being a quarterback than throwing the ball. Stan has never played, other than a few exhibition games. It's a whole different ballgame when the regular season starts, so Stan still has to prove he can do it.

I think Andre Ware is going to become one of the best quarterbacks in the league. I really haven't seen that much of him, but everyone I've talked to says he can really play. The scouts are definitely impressed with him. The only thing that could hold Andre back is playing for the Detroit Lions. They have that run-and-shoot offense, and it can take its toll on the quarterback. You're going to take a lot of shots. I just hope Andre doesn't get beat up early in his career.

Jeff George doesn't impress me all that much. The first time I saw him was last year when Illinois played Southern Cal in the season opener. I didn't like the way Jeff threw the ball. I thought he threw it side-armed. I definitely think the Colts gave up too much to get him. But you never know, it could work out for them.

Several young guys in the league are going to develop into great quarterbacks. One of them is Chris Miller of the Falcons. No matter what the defense does, he's going to throw the football. When the Redskins played the Falcons last year, we knew that our defense had to find a way to stop their passing. We were ready for Miller to throw the ball, and he was still able to do it. He passed for over 300 yards against us. We just couldn't stop him.

The Cowboys have an outstanding young quarterback in Troy Aikman. I guess he's worth all the money they paid him. Believe me, Troy has got an arm. It's a rifle. Troy is a big, talented athlete, and the Cowboys are fortunate to have him. I really think Troy is going to make a difference in that team. He's going to turn things around in Dallas.

Another young quarterback with great potential is that red-headed Huckleberry Finn kid in San Diego. Billy Joe Tolliver has a lot of ability. He reminds me of a young Sonny Jurgenson. I'm really impressed with his arm strength. I was surprised with the way he threw the ball against us last year. I remember one play where he was going down and still managed to throw a twenty-yard out. That takes a great arm.

When it comes to receivers, I think I'm a little biased, because I played with three great ones. As a group, Art Monk, Gary Clark and Ricky Sanders are the best in the league. And they're not just speed demons, they're quality receivers. They know how to get open, and they know how to beat their man. They get the job done better than any trio of receivers in the NFL.

The Raiders have the fastest set of receivers. They've got the horses with speed. Willie Gault, Tim Brown and Mervyn Fernandez can flat out fly. If the Raiders want to, they can put Ron Brown in at receiver, too. That's pure speed. They don't get any faster than those guys. Another one in that division who can really run is Jamie Miller of San Diego. He's a burner just like those guys.

A lot of people would argue that the 49ers have the best receivers in football. That's hard to dispute, but I still favor my former teammates.

Of course, Jerry Rice is by far the greatest receiver in the game. Nobody is even close to him. There's Jerry Rice and then there's the rest of the receivers in the league. Funny thing is they tried to say Jerry was too slow coming out of Mississippi Valley. They said he didn't play against great competition and couldn't make it in the pros. He's another example of the caliber of players at the small black colleges.

Jerry does whatever a receiver has to do. He can run, he knows how to beat his man, and he can catch the ball. He does it all. What's amazing to me is how Jerry gets open so much. Everyone knows San Francisco is going to try to throw to him, but he still finds an opening. You look up, and there's Jerry wide open. I can't begin to imagine how he does it. I think it's illegal.

Rice's partner in crime, John Taylor, is a lot better than he's given credit for being. I guess that's to be expected playing on the same team with Jerry Rice. But John is one of the best receivers in the NFL. When you put Jerry and John together, you've got a great opportunity to complete passes. John is another guy who went to a small black school, Delaware State, and he hasn't had any trouble adjusting to the pro game. He's also one of the best punt returners around.

As for running backs, I'll take Eric Dickerson any time. Some say he has trouble holding on to the football, that he fumbles too much. But I still like to see Eric with the football in his hands. He is unbelievably dangerous. He can break it on any run.

But without question, the best athlete in the league is Bo Jackson. He could play any position or any sport. I'd like to see Bo try defense. He would be a great defensive back. What I like best about Bo is he's a gladiator. Back in the Roman days, Bo is the guy who could have survived the lions. He's a once-in-a-lifetime type of athlete. I believe he's the greatest athlete ever. Nobody can do the things he can.

He should probably be playing basketball as well as football and baseball. I wonder if he can swim. Maybe he should try the Olympics, too.

Some people think Herschel Walker is as good as Bo. I don't. Herschel is strong and fast, but he doesn't have the agility to be a great running back. I've seen him start to turn the corner, and he literally had to come to a stop. Bo never slows down. He just plants and cuts the other way.

Another running back that I really like to see is Christian Okoye of Kansas City. He's just a train out there on the field. He'll run right over you. He has no fear. He doesn't care about linebackers and defensive ends. He doesn't care about anyone.

When he was healthy, Gerald Riggs was an outstanding running back. He was tough to stop. At full speed, Gerald was one of the great ones. Neal Anderson of Chicago still is. He combines power and speed. That makes him hard to stop.

The best pass-catching back is easily Kelvin Bryant. Nobody can do the things he does coming out of the backfield. There isn't anybody close.

Nowadays, receivers and running backs catch most of the passes. The tight ends aren't involved in the offense as much as they used to be. Things have really changed in that regard. The style of offense is more wide open and involves more speed. They just don't use a tight end anymore like we did with Tampa Bay. Jimmy Giles was a major part of the Bucs' offense. We threw to him a lot, and we went deep to him.

Tight ends usually don't catch more than fifteen or twenty passes a year. So there aren't that many who really stand out. Mark Bavaro of the Giants is an exception. He's probably the most consistent tight end in the league, and he's definitely the toughest. Mark is like a modern-day Tarzan. He can block, he can catch the football, and he can take a hit. He's a very durable and hard to bring down.

The Cardinals have a good tight end in Roy Awalt. He catches a lot of passes and is an important part of their offense. He was really effective back when Neil Lomax was their quarterback. They really worked well together.

Rodney Holman of Cincinnati is also up there as one of the best tight ends. Cleveland's Ozzie Newsome used to be one of the elite players in the league. But the Browns don't throw the ball to him much anymore. He's a prime example of how the role of the tight end has changed.

On the offensive line, the tackles who do the best job are Jim Lachey of the Redskins and Anthony Munoz of the Bengals. They're the guys I want protecting me. They're bookends. All you need is those two tackles and you can put anybody in the middle at the guards and center.

Jim is probably the best athlete I've ever seen at offensive tackle. I was shocked when he single-handedly whipped Lawrence Taylor last year. They went one-on-one and Jim won. I doubt that's ever happened before. Jim is big, strong and extremely quick. He's close to being the perfect athlete. Even though he weighs 310 pounds, he runs gracefully. He is so smooth going around the corner.

Anthony has been a consistent performer all of his life. Quick and overpowering, he never gives up a sack. He refuses to let his man get past him.

Two of the finest veteran tackles are Jim Covert of the Bears and Jackie Slater of the Rams. They've been at the top of the league for years. They've been outperforming defensive linemen for decades.

Another tackle that can get the job done consistently is Luis Sharpe of Phoenix. I remember one game when he completely shut down Dexter Manley, and that's a big job. Dexter is a super athlete, but Sharpe handled him that day.

It's hard for a quarterback to evaluate the other team's guards and center, because they're in the middle of the field and you can't see what they're doing very often. It's easy to watch the tackles on the outside.

I've never seen a better guard than Raleigh McKenzie or a better center than Jeff Bostic, who both played with me in Washington. I'll never forget the job Raleigh did on Keith Millard in the 1987 NFC championship game.

Jeff never gets enough credit for the job he does for the Redskins. I could always depend on him. Last year all of the Redskins' offensive linemen got hurt except Jeff. He kept all the young guys together and was a major reason why we started winning again. He's such a reliable performer, he has to be the best center in the game.

Picking the best offense in the NFL is the easiest choice of all. Without a doubt, the 49ers are head and shoulders above everyone else.

The 49ers are like a machine out there. Nobody executes like they do. They're unbelievable. When you put Joe Montana and Jerry Rice together, it's automatically a great offense. But the 49ers have a phenomenal supporting cast. I think they could have the best offense of all time. Nobody has every played better than they did last year, and they could do it again this season. I love to watch the 49ers. That's what football is all about.

6

No Place Like Zachary

Now that I've had some success, I realize I didn't have much growing up. At the time, I never even thought about it. I was happy, and my family was happy. We had food to eat everyday. I had clothes to wear. Even though they may have been second-hand, I had them. And I had shoes. It wasn't like I went around barefoot or anything.

I was born August 9, 1955, at Lane Memorial Hospital in Zachary, Louisiana. All my brothers and sisters were born at Charity Hospital in New Orleans. I don't really know why I was the only one born in Zachary. No one ever explained that to me. I'm the sixth of eight children of Robert and Laura Williams. They named me Douglas Lee Williams.

My home has always been Zachary and will always be Zachary. The community where I was born and raised, and where I built my own home is so small that it doesn't have a name. It's really outside of the Zachary city limits, but we always say we live in Zachary, which is about ten miles from Baton Rouge.

It was a peaceful place to grow up in and it's still a peaceful neighborhood to live in. There were a lot of older people living there, and I was always looking for something to do, so I'd volunteer to go to the store for Mr. Will or Miss Matt or Miss Jeanette or Mr. Harry. We really respected the old folks, because we were taught to. If we came home and our parents found out we had done something disrespectful, we got our ass whipped.

Growing up, my brothers and sisters and I didn't see a lot of our mom and dad. They both left for work long before we ever thought about getting up. Daddy worked construction and had to leave home at 5:30. M'Dear, which is short for Mother Dear, had to be at work at 6:30. She worked eleven years as an orderly at Lane Memorial Hospital, and then worked seventeen years as a cook in the East Baton Rouge Parish school system. M'Dear got home about five o'clock and had to feed us and get something ready for Daddy when he came home around seven. Even though my parents couldn't be with us that much, we had plenty of discipline.

We lived in a small house with three bedrooms. At that time, my oldest brother, Robert, was off at Grambling going to college, and my oldest sister, Josephine, was married and had moved out. But there were still six kids in the house. My other two sisters, Barbara Jean and Jacqueline, had one bedroom. So that left one bedroom for the four boys: Larry, Manzie, Michael and me. We had two sets of bunk beds in a ten-by-ten room. If you rolled out of your bed, you rolled into the next bed. That's how close together they were.

When I think about the house that I now have all to myself, I just wish we had that kind of room when I was a boy. But we were still fortunate. We had more than some people. It didn't bother me that we were on the free lunch program at school and got free commodities. We received powdered eggs and powdered milk. Then there was that potted meat. We used to call it horse meat. And that cheese they gave us was so hard you couldn't even slice it. You cut down on it, and it just broke apart. And the peanut butter wouldn't even spread. It just tore the bread up.

Later after I was married, I used to tell my wife Janice about the food we ate, and she didn't believe it. She thought I was making it up. I asked her if she ever ate jam sandwiches. She said, "Sure, I had jam sandwiches all the time. What kind of jelly did you use?" I had to explain that our kind of jam sandwich was different. You jammed two slices of bread together and ate it, because you didn't have anything to put in it.

We never went to the store for soft drinks and candy like most kids. We never had any money for that. What we did was mix sugar into water and call it sweet water. Every now and then on Sundays we had Kool-Aid. Sunday was the big day for us. We knew we were going to eat some rice and gravy. I'm not that big of a gravy eater today, but back then I didn't have any choice. I either liked it or I didn't eat.

I was hungry quite a bit. I remember going to people's houses, and they would offer me something. I'd say, "No thank you," even though I was hungry as a dog. My parents taught us that we weren't supposed to take things from people.

We didn't have balls to play with or things like that, so we made up our own games. We had these trees with some kind of big, hard berries growing on them, that we called cucklebugs. We'd pick some of them, take a mop handle for a bat and have a baseball game. In the house, we'd get a clothes hanger and bend it out like a basketball hoop. Then we'd stick it at the top of a door and shoot baskets with a ball made out of aluminum foil. If we didn't have a clothes hanger, we'd shoot at the curtain rods near the ceiling. We always found a way to have fun.

Even though we didn't have much, it wasn't that bad. I remember we would get the wish book of Christmas toys. They would send it to everybody in September or October, and it would get all the kids' hopes up high. Mike, Manzie and I used to sit down and talk about what we were going to get for Christmas.

"I'm going to get this bike," I'd say.

Then Mike would tell me, "Yeah, but I'm going to get this toy truck."

Heck, we would talk about it for months. And we knew all the time we weren't going to get any of those things. None of them. But you know what, when Christmas time came and we got that paper-cap pistol, we were as happy as can be. We had something to play with, so we were content. We played more Cowboys and Indians than the Big Valley. And we got a bucket full of apples and oranges. That's one time we got sick on eating apples and oranges, because we knew they weren't going to last that long.

My best time ever was getting a red Western Flyer bicycle. Can you imagine what it was like to have a bike of your own? I was in seventh grade, and my parents bought three bicycles. One for me, one for Mike and one for Manzie. They probably had them on layaway for a whole year. I couldn't believe I had my own bicycle. It was cold weather, but I didn't care—I stayed on that bike. If I got a little dirt on it, I would bring it in and wash it down. If somebody put their hands on it, I would have a fit. I wouldn't let anyone else ride it. Mine was a 26-inch bicycle, because I was a big boy. My younger brothers got 24-inch bikes. Let me tell you, that was living high.

In the summertime, we played in the woods and bayous. We picked berries and caught crawfish. I never thought a thing about walking into the woods barefoot and going through briar patches. There were snakes all around us, but I never worried about that. I looked at television shows of Tarzan swinging on vines across little streams. Believe me, I waded through more bayous than Tarzan ever dreamed about crossing. Tarzan didn't have anything on us. And his stuff was just on film. Mine was real. I never even thought about snakes until I found out some of them were poisonous. From then on, I stayed away from the woods.

When I was real young, I started playing Little League baseball, because my Daddy was probably the biggest baseball fan that ever lived in this part of the country. He played baseball in his day and wanted us to play. So he made sure we found a way to get to practices or games.

My father was a disabled veteran. Daddy was in the Army during World War II and was stationed at Pearl Harbor when the Japanese attacked. The day after the bombing, Daddy was driving a truck out there for the cleanup crew. He served four years, but had to get out with a bad back.

Daddy had two back operations, but still worked construction for something like twenty-five years. Then he had so much trouble with arthritis. His ankles, knees and hands started swelling on him, and he just couldn't work construction any more. When I was in ninth grade, my oldest brother Robert opened up a gas station, and Daddy ran it for him for a couple years. After that, he ran a nightclub out in the backwoods.

Daddy liked to gamble, and he was good at it. So a businessman by the name of Joe Holmes hired him to run his nightclub and made him a partner in the deal. They made most of their money off gambling. They would draw these huge crowds on the weekends. Some of the men would gamble and drink until they got tired and fell asleep.

Then they'd wake up and start gambling and drinking again. The place was real popular because Daddy was so well known. Everyone liked him. He just had that kind of personality. After the nightclub got going real good, Joe Holmes told Daddy that he wanted to run it himself. So he paid Daddy some money and went on his own. Business dropped off in a hurry, and the place closed down about a year later.

I was already out of college before Daddy had to slow down. He was pretty much confined to the house while I was with the Buccaneers. Then in 1983, he had to have his leg amputated. Before that, he had been very active—hunting and fishing and things like that.

One time, Daddy took me fishing and I caught the biggest fish. That was one of my greatest thrills as a boy. I was so proud when I brought that fish home, I couldn't wait to show it to M'Dear.

My parents were always concerned about me. They wanted to make sure that I was going to be all right. I was fortunate to have the kind of family that even though I eventually made some money in football, they didn't harp on that fact. They didn't say, "We need this" or "I want that." They didn't have that kind of syndrome. Their main concern was that their children were taken care of.

Daddy always gave me good advice. I remember I had been playing pro football for seven years when I decided to buy a Mercedes Benz. I'll never forget how Daddy reacted. I'm a conservative person myself, so he was surprised when I told him what I planned to do.

"Are you sure you can afford it?" Daddy asked me in his concerned way. He didn't want me to have accomplished some things and not have anything to show for it.

"Daddy, I've just paid my taxes for the year, I've got my savings, and I've got some left over," I explained. "I think it's time to do something special."

"If you think you can afford it, you go ahead," he said.

After I had signed my first pro contract, I did help my parents buy a new brick home. Daddy got a VA loan to pay for the house, and I helped them buy the land and pay the closing costs. I also furnished the house, and I bought a new car for my mother—not a Mercedes though.

M'Dear is probably the coolest mom that I've ever heard of. She doesn't get excited about little problems, and she doesn't want a lot of things. Jewelry doesn't interest her. Once I bought her a watch and a gold chain. She told me, "Thank you, baby, that's so nice." But she doesn't wear them. I also bought her a fur coat, but I've never seen her with it on. Those things aren't important to her. I don't even know what to buy for her at Christmas, so I just give her money now.

All M'Dear ever wanted was to see her children happy. She was the stronghold of the family. The pillar. We got our stability from her. Now she likes to have her grandchildren around her. I know my daughter, Ashley, is well cared for being with my mother. M'Dear treats her just like she's her own child.

M'Dear has always been supportive of what we wanted to do. When we were playing sports, she always came to the games—high school, college and the pros. M'Dear has always been there when we needed her. She has been the biggest influence on all of her children's lives.

Robert, my oldest brother, is now superintendent of middle schools in East Baton Rouge Parish. He played baseball at Grambling and pitched in the Cleveland Indians organization for three years before he hurt his arm. If it hadn't been for that, he probably would have made it to the majors.

My next oldest brother, Larry, was a heck of a baseball player. He could really swing the bat, and probably would have been a great college player or even a pro, but he didn't really want to go to school. He now works in the East Baton Rouge school system.

Manzie started at wide receiver at Jackson State, and we even played against each other once. Manzie is now a counselor at Greenwell Springs Hospital. And Mike, my youngest brother, was the starting quarterback at Grambling after I left. He threw twenty-nine touchdown passes in 1980, which was second to me in Louisiana college history. He went on to play in the Canadian Football League and got a championship ring playing with Warren Moon in Edmonton. Now Mike has his own State Farm insurance agency.

My youngest sister, Jackie, has been a schoolteacher for fourteen years. She teaches special education. Then Barbara Jean works for me, handling some of my business affairs. And Josephine has had health problems and is disabled.

My parents worked so hard that they were exhausted by the weekend. Sunday was the only day they had to rest, so we didn't get to church that much until I was older. We weren't the type to be at church every time the doors opened.

When I was in eleventh grade, I was baptized by Rev. Odell Tickles at the Greater Philadelphia Baptist Church in Zachary, and I went to church more regularly after that. I'm not an expert on the Bible or anything like that—there are some things in it I don't understand—but I'm a believer. I believe that Jesus died for us all, and by believing in him, we are saved. That's the important thing.

It wasn't easy growing up in the 1960s and 1970s in the South. Those were the days of integration, and there were hard feelings. It still bothers me today. When I went to see the movie "Mississippi Burning," I was highly upset. At one point in the movie, this Ku Klux Klan guy kicked a little boy under the chin while he was down on his knees praying. I was furious. I had a soft drink in my hand, and I just threw it at the screen and walked out of the theater.

That movie brought back so many memories. The house where I grew up is located halfway between Lemon Road and Pride-Port Hudson Road, and every Friday night, the KKK would burn a cross at each crossroad. Everybody would call out, "They're burning a cross! They're burning a cross!" If you looked down to your left, you'd see a burning cross, and if you looked down to your right, you'd see a burning cross. That really bothered us. Between those crossroads, there wasn't anybody but black people.

There was great fear in our community, especially at night. My mom always preached to us, "You'd better be here by night fall." Walking the road was dangerous. People would throw things at you. I got hit once in broad daylight. I was going to the store for my grandmother, and somebody threw a malt in my face.

At Halloween, we were afraid to go trick-or-treating, because you didn't know what was going to happen to you. Another time that everyone was careful was when LSU played Ole Miss in football. We weren't allowed on the street at all. At the time, Plank Road was a major thruway coming from Mississippi to Baton Rouge. You would see all these cars coming through with Rebel flags and bumper stickers saying, "Hell, no, I'm not forgetting." It was one of those times that parents were very worried about their children.

The integration of schools wasn't really a problem for me. What happened was they integrated our schools in my freshman year in high school in 1970, but not many white kids came to Chaneyville High School. They were supposed to go to school there, but most of them went to Central Private or Silliman Institute. They didn't want to go to school at Chaneyville. The way I looked at it, you can't run all your life. If you don't want to go to school with us, that's too bad. But someday in life, you're going to have to deal with black people. I can't think of anything in this country that you can do in which you won't eventually run into some black people. So it didn't make any sense to try to run away from us.

There was only one white guy on our football team. His name is Dale Lysone, and he's a state trooper today. He was the only one who would stick it out. When we played football, he would mix it up. He told us it didn't matter to him what color we were. I really respect that man.

Then we had another white guy, Jessie Davis, and he hung around with a black guy, Jessie Fisher. I mean they were best buddies. To me, that was great. He'd call Jessie Fisher, "Hey, ol' black ass." And Jessie would say, "Hey, ol' white boy." They were so tight that if you saw one, you always saw the other. Even today, I pass by Jessie Davis' house to see if he's outside. I just want to talk to him and see how he's doing, because I really think a lot of him. When they integrated, he came. He didn't go off somewhere else. I guess he was a lot like most of the blacks in that area. We didn't have a lot, so there wasn't any sense in running away. Just be yourself.

When you're young, a lot of things don't affect you. I guess you just don't think about it. But when you get to be older and you start thinking about what you're going to do in life, you realize being black could possibly play a role in what you want to do. Playing quarterback, I knew that I had some obstacles to overcome. But I wasn't the only one. I think being a doctor is more difficult for a black man. You've got some things to overcome. In that classroom at med school, you're a minority, and that can be tough.

It will be a long time before prejudice toward blacks ends. There's still a lot of racial tension around our community. It's not a problem with the children because they've all grown up together. They weren't even born when schools were first integrated. They don't know anything about segregated schools. But some of the adults want to keep the black-white trouble alive. They're trying to instill in the young white kids that they're better than the blacks. That's the way it is, and it should be past that point by now. But it's not. We want it to be. Sometimes we think it is. It might have gotten better, but it still isn't where we want it to be, or where it should be at this stage. And that's a shame.

Two major national events happened during my childhood. Both were assassinations. When President Kennedy was killed in 1963, I was in class at Chaneyville and remember all the teachers crying. I was only eight years old and didn't understand what was going on. I knew that the president had been shot, but I wasn't aware of what he meant to the country and particularly to the black people. It amazed me to see all my teachers crying because a white man got shot. As I grew older, I learned that to the black people in the South, John Kennedy was more than a hero. He was a symbol that they could rise up off the ground and be somebody. He showed them the way out.

It was the same way with Dr. Martin Luther King. I knew about him at that age, but I found out more and more about him as I got older. His death affected me then, but I really understand its impact now. We lost a great leader, but his message is still there for the black people. Dr. King meant so much to our people, and he means even more today to me.

About that same time, sports became very important to me. When I was real young, I liked to go out in the woods all day. But once I started playing ball, that's what I wanted to do all the time.

You were supposed to be eight before you could play Little League, but they let me start playing at seven. It took me a year before they let me pitch, which is what I really wanted to do. I can remember the first game I pitched for the Zachary Indians, a team that was in an all-black league. Nobody had scored going into the bottom of the fifth inning, and we played only five innings. I had come in to relieve in the third inning and was still pitching, and the other team loaded up the bases. The guy at the plate was Tim Butler. He was a real big boy. I was only eight, and he must have been ten or eleven. Tim hit a grand slam, and they won the game 4-0. I cried like a baby after that game.

I guess you could say I was a crybaby when it came to losing. I just hated to lose anything. But after that first game, I remember our coach, Milton Lee, came up and told me, "I don't want to coach no crybaby. If you're going to cry, you're going to have to find some place else to play." Later, I found out he told Daddy that he was glad I cried, because that showed how much I wanted to win.

As I got older, I became one of the better Little League pitchers around. Robert helped me a lot with my pitching. I developed a curveball, and I was really tough to hit.

We won most of our games in Little League. In my last game, I was eleven and was the starting pitcher for an All-Star team. I pitched the first nine innings, and with the game tied, 1-1, they made me stop, because of a rule that a Little League player can pitch only nine innings a week. The other team ended up beating us, 2-1, in fifteen innings.

When I moved up to Pony League, I didn't do as well. You had to move back and pitch from the mound, and I wasn't that strong. I was just a little, skinny kid. My curveball worked pretty well, but my fastball wasn't the greatest. In high school, I was a pretty decent pitcher, and I kept getting stronger and stronger.

In my senior year in high school, I started playing American Legion baseball in the summer. I played the first year they allowed blacks in the league. There were three of us on the Sealtest Ice Cream team: John Arthur Stewart, Sherman Floyd and me. It was tough. Most of the players didn't want to accept us. You're talking about a time when the tension of integration was high. It was a difficult time.

An incident that stands out in my mind occurred at one of our practices. I was on third base at the time, and we had a player named Carey Carpenter. He was in the dugout, and I didn't know what was going on, but for some reason he said nigger. I didn't know if he was referring to me or not, but he said something about a nigger. I mean this was a teammate of mine, so I was really upset. I went over to the dugout, and he said, "I'm sorry." But that was my teammate. We're playing together on the same team, and he's talking about niggers. Right then, I realized what I was up against.

But that was just the beginning. The league was played in Denham Springs, and that's where the Grand Wizard of the Ku Klux Klan used to live. They called me every name you can imagine. I was called nigger, black lizard and a bunch of other things. One time, we were playing a team from Denham Springs, and I slid into home. The catcher got the ball and jumped down hard on me. It felt like he almost killed me. My back was aching as I got up, but I made up my mind that I was going to get him back. Later, I was playing second base, and that same guy tried to steal second on us. Our catcher Leo McClure threw the ball to me, and I caught it and slapped that guy across the head with my glove as hard as I could. They had to come get him off the field.

Leo's father came to every game that he could, and he was the driving force in helping me to keep my sanity out there. He used to invite us to his house and treat us really nice. Mr. McClure never talked from a black-white standpoint. He always treated us the same as everybody else. We'd sit at his kitchen table and drink Kool-Aid or have something to eat.

Leo and all of his brothers were always really good to me, too. When others would call me names, Leo would come up and tell me, "That's all right, Doug. Don't pay any attention to them. Just throw the ball." When things were going well, they'd hug me. We became real good friends.

By my senior year, I was throwing the ball hard and had become a dominant pitcher and some scouts came out to see me pitch. One of them wanted me to go play in an instructional league in Kansas City. But Robert was dead set against it. He had played in the minor leagues and he knew what it was all about. Not many players ever make it to the big leagues. Robert thought that would be the wrong move for me. He wanted me to go on to college and play baseball and football.

When I finally did get to Grambling, I was on a baseball and football scholarship, and I was really looking forward to playing college baseball. But the season conflicted with spring football, and Coach Robinson gave me an ultimatum, either work out with the football team or give it up and just play baseball. I chose spring football practice, and that was the end of my baseball career.

My first chance to play football as a kid came in my eighth-grade year at Chaneyville. The eighth-grade team just practiced on plays and had scrimmage games. They put me at quarterback right away, and that was the only position I ever wanted to play.

But the next year, Robert became an assistant coach at Chaneyville, and he made me play linebacker and quarterback. I didn't really want to play football anyway, and I definitely didn't want to play linebacker. Basically, I didn't like contact. I liked baseball and loved basketball, but Robert insisted that I play football. So I went out for quarterback, and he made me play middle linebacker. He just wanted to toughen me up, because he thought that you have to be tough to survive in this world.

When I was young, I always tried to hang around Robert. Every time he came home from school or from playing minor league baseball, he would spend time with me and take me around places with him. I was a little nerd who followed him all over. Then after Robert became a teacher and coach at Chaneyville, he made sure that I did what it took to get my high school diploma. It was important to him that I was headed in the right direction. He's played a major role in everything I've been able to accomplish.

Even when I was a little boy, he dogged me. He made me catch his pitches that were going 90 or 95 miles per hour. He made me play tackle football against my brothers. We didn't even have a football, so we used a small Clorox jug. It would be so cold, and we'd still be out there tackling each other.

I didn't really like hitting people, so linebacker wasn't the position for me. I thought it was more fun to run away from the defense. In my freshman season at Chaneyville, I started at free safety, and we were playing the Second Ward from Edgard. Their quarterback was Terry Robiskie, who later played running back for LSU and in the NFL. Second Ward also had this real big running back. On one play, he broke through the line and was in the open. I came up and hit him head on and took a fierce shot. I came off the field and told my coach I didn't want any part of defense anymore.

It took a couple years before I finally got a chance to play quarterback for the team. I was so small at first that I couldn't even see over the center's head. As a freshman, I was only five-feet-five. Then I started to grow like a bean pole. Over the summer, I grew six inches, and then I was big enough to play. But I still didn't start, because we had some older guys ahead of me, even though I probably had the best arm out there. On Thursdays, the day before our games, we always had a light warmup and passed the ball around. I could always throw it farther than anyone else.

In my junior year, Wendell Braxton was the starting quarterback, but he injured an ankle early in the season. They made me the starting quarterback, and I never gave it up. Wendell was a good athlete, so they moved him to defensive back, wide receiver and running back, and I remained at quarterback. We were having a good season and earned a playoff spot pretty early. But in the last game of the season, we were playing Southern Lab, and I broke my ankle. We lost the game, 26-13, and I couldn't play anymore that season. Actually, I was glad I didn't get to play, because Wesley Ray High School beat the heck out of us in the playoffs, something like 52-14.

By my senior year, I was getting much bigger and stronger and I started to get some attention from the colleges. It helped when I had a good season, throwing for 1,800 yards and 22 touchdowns. But what really got me interested in college football was watching a Southern University game.

I remember Southern was playing Tennessee State which had a quarterback named ''Jefferson Street'' Joe Gilliam. He was a senior, and everybody was talking about what a great quarterback he was. I couldn't wait to see him play. I wanted to get as close to him as I could, so at halftime I stood down by the fence and watched him walk by. It was surprising to see how small he was. I couldn't believe this skinny guy was really Jefferson Street Joe. At the time, I was about 6-2, 180 pounds, and I thought, ''Shoot, if he can play college football, I know I can play. I'm bigger than him.''

Right then, I made up my mind that I wanted to play quarterback in college. Before that, my plans were to go to school, get a degree and become a coach like my brother Robert. I wanted to be just like him. But watching Joe Gilliam that night made me realize I could play college football and become a coach, too. From that time on, I was convinced I was going to be a quarterback.

7

Playing for a Legend

Late one November night, M'Dear woke me up and got me out of bed. She said Coach Eddie Robinson was on the phone and wanted to talk to me. I was a senior at Chaneyville, and somebody had told Coach Rob about me. I couldn't believe it when I found out Eddie Robinson wanted to recruit me. You're talking about a legend, and he wanted to speak to me about playing for him. I was overwhelmed.

As a boy, I watched all the highlights of Grambling football on TV every Sunday morning and read all about the things that Coach Rob's teams had done. Most people considered Grambling to be the black's Notre Dame. Coach Rob had already been at Grambling more than thirty years when he recruited me. By then, he was well on his way to 300 wins. Today, he's the winningest coach in the history of college football with a 358-125-15 record in forty-seven years. There's no doubt in my mind that Coach Rob is the greatest coach of all time. And he's got the numbers to show it, too. That's stats. That's using the American system. No disrespect to Bear Bryant, but Coach Rob is the greatest coach ever. Some people will argue that he coached in the smaller division, but the man played whomever he could play.

Coach Rob has taken his teams all over the country to play—

places like Yankee Stadium, the L.A. Coliseum, Giants Stadium, Aloha Stadium, the Cotton Bowl and even Tokyo. Now everyone knows about him. Not everyone, though, realizes how many players he has sent to the NFL. The first black player in the league, Tank Younger, played for him at Grambling. Since then, Coach Rob has sent almost 300 players into the NFL.

My community is full of Grambling supporters. We had some people who had already gone there to play sports. My brother, Robert, had gone there. Henry Dyer, who used to play with the Los Angeles Rams and Washington Redskins, went from Chaneyville High School to play for Coach Rob at Grambling. Leroy Carter, who later coached at Scotlandville High School in Baton Rouge, played football at Grambling. So our community had a lot of ties with Grambling. Everyone around there thought Grambling was the only school that gave people from our community a fair shot. When Henry Dyer and Leroy Carter were being recruited out of Chaneyville, Southern coach A.W. Mumford said he could get players like that a dime a dozen. People in our community were offended, and that made them even more supportive of Grambling. To me, there was no better school in the country than Grambling.

The thing I remember most about my first talk with Coach Rob was that he didn't make any promises. Some coaches would tell you, ''Come to our school and you can start. You can do this and you can do that.'' Coach Rob just told me that they would give me the opportunity to play. The rest was up to me. I thought that was great. All that a man can ask for is an opportunity.

At that time, Southern was recruiting me, too. But Charlie Bates was the coach then, and they ran that darn wishbone. Plus, Southern was recruiting Terry Robiskie. Everybody wanted him, and it was rumored that Southern had offered Terry a car. Pete Shaw, who was Southern's offensive coordinator, came to my house and brought me a fruit basket. I wasn't about to go to Southern for a fruit basket to run the wishbone.

None of the white schools contacted me during high school. The only contact I ever received from LSU came after I had already gone to Grambling for a year. The summer after my first year in college, I was playing American Legion baseball, and Coach Jim Smith from

LSU called my brother Robert and inquired about me going to LSU on a baseball scholarship. Robert told him it was too late because I was a redshirt freshman at Grambling.

It really didn't matter who else was recruiting me after Coach Rob called. I didn't tell him right away, but it was over with. Anybody could have come and offered me a scholarship, and it wouldn't have mattered. I knew where I was going.

I went up to Grambling early in the summer of 1973. It was the worst summer of my life. First of all, I had never been away from home for any length of time. I can remember sitting in front of the union with three other guys. I had a home boy, James Smith, with me. We had both played ball at Chaneyville. That day, we were all so lonely. I remember these two little birds just flew down in front of me and started playing in the dust. That's what we did that afternoon, watched the birds play in the dust. I was so homesick that I wanted to leave right then and come home.

I stayed through the summer hoping things would get better once the season started. It didn't. They told me I would be redshirted, and I was devastated. It was the first time in my life that I wouldn't be playing. That was a big letdown for me.

What Coach Rob did was let me stay with the team and work as a statistician for games. That's how I got to travel with the team. I only practiced with the scout team. They already had the starter, Joe Comaux. And the other guy, Terry Brown, was a highly recruited quarterback out of Captain Shreve in Shreveport. Terry had led Captain Shreve to the state championship, and a lot of schools recruited him. Naturally, he got the first shot ahead of me. I was just a country boy with some potential. I couldn't really argue with Coach Rob when he decided to redshirt me. I was up there, and I saw the situation.

That first semester was miserable. They tried to make me feel part of the team, but that wasn't enough for me. I was dejected. For a long time, I thought I was going to transfer to Southern. Coach Rob and I had a meeting about it, and I told him I was ready to transfer.

"You may think you want to, but you're not going to," Coach Rob said. "We believe you can help us. We think you're going to be our quarterback one day."

That was hard to imagine when we had a starter who was a junior and the backup was a freshman. I asked myself, "How many years am

I going to play here? One?'' It looked like I might have to wait four years to play one season. But Coach Rob convinced me that I should stick it out.

Since I wasn't playing football that first semester, I didn't have much incentive to hit the books. Going to school didn't appeal to me, and I ended up with a 1.5 grade point average for the semester which put me on academic probation. When my grades were sent home over the break, Daddy got a look at them, and he was mad. He told my mom, ''Well, shoot, let him get a job.'' That was his way of saying it was time to take care of myself.

At that time, I wasn't too anxious to get a job and go to work. Get a job? I didn't want any job. So I went right back to school and got serious about my academics. I got a 2.5 the next semester and after that, I never had any trouble with school.

That spring, I got to practice with the varsity. I thought I had a real good spring. In fact, I think I played better than any other quarterback. But going into the fall, I was still the No. 3 man.

It got more frustrating when we lost one of our early games. Coach Rob went back and forth with Joe and Terry. I was third team and kept thinking, ''Neither one of them is doing anything and they're still not playing me. I must not be any good.''

I was really down on myself. Finally, I decided to quit the team. I just wasn't going to come to practice anymore. I missed one day, and then the next day I was up in my room when Coach Fred Hobdy came to see me. He was the basketball coach, but he was also an assistant for football. He came up to the room, and I was looking at ''The Big Valley'' on TV.

''What the hell do you think you're doing?'' Coach Hobdy shouted.

''Coach, I'm not playing anymore.''

''We gave you a scholarship. You're going to play! Come on out of here!''

Coach Hobdy was a good friend of my brother Robert, so he wanted to help me out. He went with me down to the locker room and stayed there while I got dressed.

When I finally got out on the field, practice was almost over. I was moping around. I thought I'd pull one of those Duane Thomas moves on them. I wouldn't say nothing to nobody. I thought that might hurt somebody if I didn't talk to them. So I didn't say anything the rest of practice. The next day, I went back and didn't say anything again.

But after a while, I started to realize if you don't say anything to anybody, nobody's going to say anything to you. I would be left out in the cold. Coach Rob knew what I was going through. He just left me alone and let me sort things out.

I was still sulking when the team was getting ready for that week's game at Prairie View. I said to myself, "This is one time I won't have to go." So I didn't pack my bag, it was just sitting empty in my locker. But somebody must have told one of the trainers to pack it, because it was ready to go.

On Friday morning, the buses were out in the parking lot real early, because we had to drive to Dallas for the game. I could hear the diesel engines roaring, but I didn't get up. I had made up my mind that I wasn't going. If they weren't going to play me, there wasn't any point in going on the road with them.

Once again, Coach Hobdy came to get me. I was still in bed when he walked into my room. He just told me to hurry up and get dressed, because the whole team was waiting on me. I put some clothes on, got on the bus and ended up playing in my first college game.

By then, the team had started to play well and had won three games in a row. We were killing Prairie View in the third quarter when I got the call. But that didn't matter, I was just glad to finally get a chance to play. Everything went great. I completed 6 of 7 and threw my first TD pass. It was a TD to Sammy White. I've still got the ball in my house today.

Since I went in so early in the second half, I expected to play quite a bit. But after one series, they took me out and put Terry Brown back in. I was thinking that they put Terry back in because he was the No. 2 quarterback and they didn't want me to outdo him.

The next week, we played Tennessee State, which is always a big game for us. Joe Comaux broke his wrist and had to come out. They put Terry in for a while, but he couldn't move the team. So I got my second turn. I led us on a long scoring drive, and we went on to win the game, 21-0. That put me in line to move up to No. 1.

Our next game was with Mississippi Valley, and Coach Rob wouldn't name a starting quarterback until the day of the game. He told us that the coaches voted on me to be the starter. I never gave it up, and the rest is history. We won or shared the Southwestern Athletic Conference championship four straight years and ended up winning thirty-five out of forty games. That's the only time Grambling won four straight conference championships.

Against Valley, we had to really struggle to win. The Delta Devils had a heck of a quarterback by the name of Parnell Dickinson. As a matter of fact, the Tampa Bay Bucs drafted him in 1976. He played one season for them and still lives in Tampa. Let me tell you, Parnell could play football. Our defensive back Mike Harris made two diving plays to break up passes and save the game for us. That was a tough ballgame. David Dixon, our best running back, really had a good day. I had a good day myself, and we won 21-14. From then on, I knew I belonged there.

That stretched our winning streak to five with four games left. Our toughest game came against Jackson State to decide the SWAC championship. They had Walter Payton at tailback at that time. I had a real good game with two TD passes, and we beat them 26-13.

That was also the first year of the Bayou Classic between Grambling and Southern. It was played in Tulane Stadium in New Orleans. We had won eight straight by then and were really on a roll. Final score: 21-0—us. Later that same month, we got another chance to play in Tulane Stadium, this time in the Pelican Bowl. We played South Carolina State, which had Harry Carson on its team. We beat them 27-7 and finished the season at 11-1. It was a great way to start my college career.

In 1975, we had a real good senior class with players like Sammy White and James Hunter. Sammy went on to the Minnesota Vikings and was Rookie of the Year in 1976. We had some excellent athletes on that team. Our best game of that season was a comeback win over Tennessee State. Anytime you beat Tennessee State it's a big win, but this one was really tough. They had us down 14-0 in Nashville. I threw two TD passes in the game, and Sammy caught the winning TD pass late in the fourth quarter to give us a 27-25 win.

We would have had an undefeated season if it hadn't been for Jackson State. They beat us 27-7, but we still ended up winning the SWAC championship.

We finished 10-1, but the season didn't end well for me. During our 31-17 win over Southern in the Bayou Classic, I hurt my knee seriously. On November 29, I had reconstructive surgery. I'll never forget that day.

Back in those days, knee surgery wasn't anything like it is today. The doctors cut me, fixed the knee and then put a sixty-pound cast on my leg. They told me to stay off my feet for six weeks. I never moved my leg, so it got real stiff from staying in one place. If I had the same surgery today, they would put a hinge cast on, and I would be up and around right away. Everything is flexible when you use a hinge cast. After I got that big cast off, I lost a lot of speed. I went from a 4.6 in the 40 to about a 4.75, which still wasn't bad for a quarterback.

I then faced eight or nine months of rehab. I didn't participate in spring practice—all I did was work on my knee, trying to get it stronger. I had a brace, but refused to wear it. My feeling was if I got hit, I wouldn't be able to play anymore, so I didn't want that brace slowing me down.

At the start of my junior season, I was just starting to get to full strength, and we were kind of in a rebuilding year, having lost so many seniors. We played at Alcorn State in the opener, and they had the best defense I had ever seen. They beat us 24-0. It was my only shutout in college, and the only game in which I didn't throw at least one TD pass. I wasn't that down because I knew I had just come off knee surgery. Actually, I was happy to be back in the game. It gave me some confidence that I would be able to return. I got hit, I got sacked, and I was all right. That first game showed me that my knee had recovered. That was such a relief.

The next week, we traveled to Philadelphia to play Temple. They scored on about a 40-yard TD pass in the last thirty-three seconds to beat us 31-30. That put us at 0-2.

At that point, I really had to be a leader. That's something I never really had to be in the past. Sammy, James and Dwight Scales were all gone. They had been our leaders. Since I was the quarterback, I had to take over. Then I really learned what it was like to be a leader. I started to take control.

After the losses to Temple and Alcorn, we turned it around and won eight of our final nine games. We were playing just like we used to play, and I was feeling great. We beat Jackson State and Southern, finished 8-3 and shared the SWAC championship with Alcorn.

My senior year was hectic because of all the hype about winning the Heisman Trophy, being All-American and all that. Collie Nicholson, Grambling's sports information director, did a good job of hyping and selling Doug Williams. Collie was a guy who knew all the media and knew how to build somebody up. If a player was 6-2, Collie would say he was 6-4. He sent out lots of information and press releases on me. He didn't send out posters like some schools, because Grambling didn't have that kind of money. Still, it was a big deal to be promoting a Grambling player for the Heisman Trophy.

I never even dreamed of winning the Heisman, because I understood. Being a black quarterback from a black college, the chances were slim and none for me. But Coach Rob believes in America, and he always says anything is possible if you live in America. The Heisman stuff really wasn't for me, it was for Coach. He wanted to keep the dream alive.

The 1977 season was another good one for us. We were playing well and had a chance to go unbeaten. But we lost to Tennessee State, at Tennessee State, in the driving rain. We had some bad breaks—one touchdown called back and two dropped TD passes—and they won the game 21-7. But we went undefeated in the SWAC and won our fourth straight conference championship. That meant a lot to me, because the SWAC is the most important thing for Grambling and we won it every year.

I'll never forget my last game with Coach Rob. We were in Tokyo and had a chance to be rematched with Temple. Late in the game, we were behind 32-28 and had the ball on our 15-yard line. At that time, I had 38 touchdown passes for the season, and the NCAA record was 39 set by Dennis Shaw. We marched down inside the 10 and I called time out with less than a minute left.

On the sidelines, Coach Rob told me, "We've got four shots to throw it in the end zone and get a TD." Coach was thinking about breaking the record and about winning the game. He had a lot of things on his mind.

"No, Coach, we're going to run it," I told him.

"What?"

"We're going to run the ball, Coach. It's open."

Temple was rushing only two linemen and dropping nine people back into a zone. Everyone in the ballpark was looking for a pass. The Japanese wanted me to throw another TD pass. They were loving the

game. But it was just too open on the inside. Even though we had our
backup tailback Floyd Womack in the game, I thought we could run for
a TD. I told Coach Rob that we should leave Floyd in, so they wouldn't
expect anything.

I called a 37 sweep, and believe me, nobody came close to touch-
ing Floyd. Everybody was playing pass. He went in standing up, and
we won the game 35-32.

Earlier that week, they had announced that Earl Campbell of
Texas had won the Heisman Trophy. I finished fourth, and they didn't
even invite me to the dinner in New York. But I got the only award I
needed in our locker room after the Temple game.

Coach Rob called the team together and made a statement: ''Regardless of what anybody says, the Heisman Trophy winner is here in
this room.''

That was a heck of a compliment. I'll never forget what Coach
Rob said. I thought about all the great players who had come to Gram-
bling to play for him, and he was saying I deserved to be the Heisman
Trophy winner. That really meant a lot to me.

When I played my last game for Coach Rob, I had set an NCAA
record with 93 career touchdown passes and had thrown for 8,411
yards, second highest ever at the time. I consider that last game to be
the highlight of my career. It wasn't so much winning the game as it
was the comeback. To go eighty-five yards in the last three minutes.
To never quit, never say die. That's what Grambling and Coach Rob
are all about.

Coach Rob made me believe that I could be a professional quarterback. In my junior year, I was playing well again after the knee surgery, and I began to think I might get a chance to play pro ball. Joe
Gilliam was playing a little bit at the time, and James Harris was still
playing some. I thought the NFL might be ready for another black
quarterback.

For a long time, I had battled with the thought that no matter how
good I became, I wouldn't get a chance to play pro ball, because the
NFL had that black quarterback syndrome. But I didn't think about
that later in my career, and Coach Rob was the reason why. He was
always such a positive individual.

Coach Rob's ability to motivate players has always amazed me.
He's just a great talker, and he can sell you on anything. He's so posi-

tive and so persuasive, I think he could sell ice and a lawn mower to an Eskimo. That's what kind of salesman he is. To witness his pregame speeches is to really appreciate him. You have to watch him cry. I've seen him cry many times, and he's so good at it, it makes you want to cry. After you hear one of his speeches, you're so revved up and pumped up you want to run through the wall.

When we played Southern University, he could really get us up for the game. He'd be holding his head down and fighting back the tears. Then he'd finally say something like this: "Dammit, I remember when they used to walk in here and stomp up on us. Brother, they would just warm up on Grambling. They didn't give a damn about us. They didn't respect us."

Then Coach Rob would weep a little more, and look around the room and say, "You all don't want to play. You're going to get the hell beat out of you. You'd better be ready, because they don't respect us. They just don't respect us."

Our guys would be so quiet, and they'd have that look in their eyes like they wanted to kill. When Coach Rob finished, they couldn't get out of the room fast enough. They were ready to destroy.

What I respect about Coach more than anything else is how he prides himself on his players who graduate. That's the most important thing to him. All these new rules that the NCAA has aren't needed at Grambling. Football players get their degrees there. Coach Rob makes sure of that.

Coach Rob would get up at six o'clock in the morning and walk up and down the hall ringing a cowbell to make sure the guys would get up, go to breakfast and then go to class. He always said he was waking us up to go to breakfast, but his theory was if you get up for breakfast, you're going to go to class. But if you don't get up at all, you'll sleep late, miss two or three classes, and it will be lunch time before you get going.

Coach Rob always preached about being a good American, and the only way to do that is to secure a good education. He really placed more importance on education than football. He didn't just talk about it. He did it. His philosophy was that he'd rather have an A student who is a C football player than a C student who is an A football player.

It bothered Coach when someone missed class. We had this setup where you had to run the stadium steps ten times if you missed a class. And you had to run after practice, not before. So after a hard day of practice, you didn't want to be running the stadium steps. He did other little things like that to encourage us to go to class. And even today, if there's a guy who has finished playing and still wants to get a degree, Coach Rob will find a way to get that guy in school and finish up his degree.

More than anything else, Coach Rob prepared me for the world and what it has to offer. He's so patriotic. I don't know of anyone else who believes so strongly in America. And he instills that belief in his players.

Coach Rob helped me to be able to remain positive in a negative situation. I think that's the only way I could have survived what I've been through in football and in my personal life. He knew what I was up against being a black quarterback going into the NFL. He was close to James Harris, so he knew what James had been through. And I respect James, too, because he never tried to sour me on the league. Everything I learned, I had to learn on my own. He didn't want me to go into it looking for prejudice or racism. And Coach Rob was the same way. Never once did he say to me, "Well, James encountered this, and this is what you're going to be confronted with." Instead, he always said to me, "Doug, you've got to be a man about things. You've got to be able to handle what is thrown your way. Over the years, you'll have to cope with it. You'll have to be able to talk to the press and get your point across."

Cooperating with the media was always important to Coach Rob. We talked about that a lot during my senior year when I got all the Heisman hype. He believed that you have to be ready to talk whenever they pop that microphone in front of your face.

Coach Rob prepared me for the mental aspects of football and life. Not that he brought me in a room and said, "This is what you've got to do, Doug." When he wanted to get a point across to me, he would say it to the whole team and everyone could apply it to his own situation.

He's just a very positive, caring individual. I became a better football player and a complete person under him. I've been fortunate to have been graced with his presence in my life. From that standpoint, I'm the luckiest man in the world.

8

Janice

So much happened during my second year at Grambling. I finally got a chance to play football and became the starting quarterback. We won the conference championship and went to a bowl game. That's also the year I met Janice.

I'll never forget the day I saw her for the first time. Ricky Grant, who was my roommate and runnin' partner at the time, and I were at the library. We used to go there all the time to read the *Baton Rouge Morning Advocate*. That's how we kept up with all the things going on back home. Mainly, we read about the high school games and things like that. Now Janice used to go to the library all the time with her friends, too. I remember sitting in there reading the newspaper and when I looked up, I saw Janice for the first time. I told Ricky, "I really like her. I've got to meet that girl."

What I'll never forget about seeing her that first time was her smile. Janice Goss had a smile that was second to none. When I looked at her face, it just made me feel good. She was a very attractive young lady. Breathtaking. Eye catching. And I thought I had pretty good eyes at that time anyway.

It was a day later when I finally said something to Janice. We talked a little bit, and I ended up walking her to her dorm. We became good friends and saw a lot of each other. It wasn't long before she was my girlfriend, and we dated for the next four years.

Our first date was going down to the Village to get a hamburger. The Village is in downtown Grambling right on Main Street. You've got about three or four little hamburger places, the Collegiate Shop, the barber shop, and Penny's Cafe. That's it in Grambling.

But just taking Janice out for a hamburger was a big deal back then. We didn't have any money for hamburgers in those days. Money was scarce as hen's teeth. I was lucky because I got some money from Daddy being a disabled veteran. I had an orange Volkswagen Bug to drive and a little spending money in my pocket. But I didn't flaunt it. My big treat was going to Burger King on Sundays. That was the one day I didn't eat in the cafeteria. Once Janice and I started dating, we would usually go out to eat on Sundays. We mainly just got together on the weekends, because I was busy with football and she was pledging the Delta Sigma Theta sorority. Sometimes we went to see a movie on campus. But most of the time we'd just get together and talk. Believe me, there wasn't a lot to do at Grambling.

Janice was a real, down-to-earth country girl from Gainesville, Georgia. She was a little shy, but had a great personality. She just smiled all the time and there was nothing like her smile in the world.

We never talked about sports or anything like that, so I never did bother to tell her that I was on the football team. She eventually found out on her own. That sounds funny, but we were interested in other things.

Truthfully, I don't ever like to talk about football. I've never been one to try to impress people with what I do. You shouldn't have to tell people that you're this or you're that. I think you should just be yourself and let them make up their own mind about you.

Janice and I had been dating for weeks before she found out I played quarterback for the football team. I didn't want her to like me because of what I did, I wanted her to like me as a person. She even went to the games and didn't know I was playing. Everyone went to the football games at Grambling. But Janice wasn't into football, and I guess she wasn't really paying attention to the game. Even after we were married and I had been playing pro football for several years, she didn't pay much attention to football. It just didn't interest her at all.

Janice finally learned I played football when my mother came to one of our games in October of my redshirt freshman season. M'Dear and some of her friends were waiting for me outside the locker room. When I came out, Janice just happened to be walking by with some of her friends and was really surprised when she saw me walk out of the locker room.

"You didn't tell me you played football, Doug!" she exclaimed, her mouth flying wide open.

I just started laughing about it. I told her, "Yeah, I do play football." Then I introduced her to my mother. We never did say much more about it.

Most of the time, Janice and I just talked about school and friends. Just everyday things. We just enjoyed each other's company. I guess when you first meet a person, you're always curious about the other people they've been dating. She told me about the boyfriend she had at home, but at that time they weren't getting along. I didn't have a girlfriend at that time. I had a girlfriend my first year at Grambling, but Janice was the first girl I ever met that I felt there was a future in our relationship. I knew right away she was somebody I was very interested in. It was love at first sight. I just knew she was somebody I could spend the rest of my life with.

It didn't faze Janice that other girls were interested in me. Being a name athlete on campus, you always ran across girls. I had plenty of girls who wanted to talk to me, and that did not upset Janice. All she wanted to know was that she was my girlfriend.

Janice was a very unselfish person. She didn't have to be right beside me all the time. She gave me some freedom. She wasn't the type to flaunt herself and be a showboat.

M'Dear was crazy about Janice. She loved Janice right from the start. I took Janice home to meet my family, and she had a great time. She was just like my sister Jackie. They have great personalities and get along with everyone. They just relate to people so well. The kids clung to Janice. They thought the world of her. She fit right in with my family and loved it in Zachary.

My mother really liked the fact that Janice wanted to learn how to cook red beans. M'Dear loves to show people how to make red beans. Nobody makes them like my mom, but Janice got pretty good at it. She had plenty of practice, making them for me about every week at school.

The year after I met Janice, I hurt my knee and was really down about it. I thought my football career was over. After the surgery, I had to spend a week in the hospital in Monroe and another week in the campus infirmary. Janice wouldn't leave my side at the hospital, even though it was late in the school year and she needed to be studying.

Janice made sure I got whatever I wanted. If I was hungry, she went out and bought me whatever I asked for, whether it was hamburgers or shrimp. She took real good care of me. I'd take my medicine and fall asleep, and when I'd wake up, she'd still be sitting there. I used to tell her that she needed to go study, but she wouldn't listen to me.

There was a ten o'clock curfew in the infirmary, and they were real strict about it. But I remember the head nurse, Mrs. Brown, finally gave up on trying to get Janice to leave by ten. She just told her, "Look, you make sure you give him his medicine before he goes to sleep." And then she would leave us alone.

Being in that hospital and knowing that my football days might be over was the worst feeling in the world. But Janice wouldn't let me stay down. She really lifted up my spirits.

Janice was an outstanding student. Her major was economics, and she had about a 3.5 grade point average for her first year. But she almost got in trouble with her grades because she spent so much time at the hospital with me. Her GPA dropped to around 2.3 that year. She picked it back up the next year and ended up graduating with honors.

Janice helped me with my studies sometimes, and was a good influence on my taking academics seriously. When I was doing my student teaching, she really helped me, because I had a lot of papers to do. She made sure I had my lesson plans ready. And if she was busy, she found somebody else to help me.

Of course, Coach Rob made an impact on me as far as education, too. He talked so much about the value of getting a good education, so I knew I needed to make the effort. I had an eight o'clock class every morning for five straight years, and I never once missed it if we were in town.

Another person who stressed academics to me was Bessie McKinney. She had been my brother Robert's advisor when he went to

Grambling. I think she was the best thing that ever happened to Doug Williams as a student. She worked in the physical education department and became my counselor. But she also became my mom away from home. Before I met Janice, if I wanted red beans, Miss McKinney cooked red beans. She treated me like her son. And what really helped me was she always made sure I was working toward my degree.

I can't believe how much energy Miss McKinney has. She's just a little lady, about five-feet-two, if that tall. But she's so vivacious. She will always tell you what's on her mind, whether you like it or not. She doesn't pull any punches. If she can help and you want her to help you, she'll help you. But you've got to want it. Miss McKinney has helped a lot of athletes and a lot of other students at Grambling by teaching them what it takes to graduate.

Miss McKinney put me in the right classes and made sure I didn't have too many hours. Her main concern was not that I stayed eligible to play football, but that I attained a degree from Grambling State University. She did so much for me. I still call her today, and she still gives me good advice.

Getting that college degree was important because I knew it would open up so many doors to me. I really wanted to be a coach, and I had to have a degree to get a chance to coach. That's what I really wanted to do. Playing professional football was like a bonus. If it worked out, fine. If not, I knew I could become a coach. I never dreamed of making a lot of money and driving a Mercedes. I always thought I'd have a Chevrolet or a LTD and spend my time coaching youngsters.

After that first semester, I didn't have any problems with my grades. I finished school with a 2.8 grade point average, and I graduated on time with a B.S. in Health and Physical Education.

Janice and I graduated at the same time. I remember the graduation ceremony was on Mother's Day in 1978. That diploma really meant a lot to me, and to M'Dear. I think a college degree is the best thing you can give your mother. That's what they look forward to, seeing their children grow up, go to school and get a college diploma. M'Dear wanted all of her kids to be successful. That was the most important thing in her life.

It was a great Mother's Day for M'Dear. I had just been drafted in the first round by the Tampa Bay Buccaneers and now she was watching her son go across the stage to pick up his diploma. It meant a lot to me to be able to hand my mother a college diploma. It was a great day for all of us.

Being drafted in the first round was really a thrill for me. I had no doubt I would be drafted, it was just a question of what round and where I would be going. I wanted to go to New Orleans, because it was close to home and I had followed the Saints. I really wanted to be a part of the New Orleans Saints.

No black quarterback had ever been drafted in the first round, so obviously I wasn't sure I would be taken in the first round. When I got the call from the Bucs, I was naturally elated. It was a new franchise, and I knew I would get a chance to play. I liked Coach John McKay, and I had seen his teams at Southern Cal play. Tampa looked like a great place for Doug Williams to play pro football. I was ready to go.

Janice and I didn't get married right away. But we had spent four years together at college, and it was evident we were going to get married. I knew I was going to walk away with my college sweetheart. It was only a matter of time.

Even though we waited to get married, we were always there for each other. We had never talked about getting married; it was just understood that we would. Janice never said she was disappointed that we didn't get married right away. She knew she was No. 1 with me. Not one time did she voice discouragement or disappointment at not being married.

After graduation, I went to Tampa and she went home to Georgia. She got a good position working for Liberty Mutual as an underwriter, and she always came to visit me and called me all the time. We talked almost every night. We never had a falling-out during that whole time. She always remained my girlfriend, there was never any doubt about that. She came to see me in Tampa whenever she felt like it and she went back home when she was ready.

After a few years, I decided it was time to get married. I had played pro football for a while and had accomplished some things. I had bought my first house and was all settled down. To me, it was time to get married and start a family.

Janice and I were talking on the phone one night, and I told her, "Janice, let's get married." She said, "That's OK with me." It wasn't that big of a thing with us. It was just a matter of deciding when to do it.

Everybody else knew Janice and I were going to get married, too. But nobody interfered in our business, even though I'm sure they wondered when it was going to happen. Our wedding was held on April 17, 1982. Janice was finally with me in Tampa and we were happy.

Those were great days for us. At last, I was with the lady whom I had loved for eight years, and it was a great feeling. When you've spent that much time with somebody, you really know each other. You know what you've got. I couldn't have been happier. We were so much alike. We had the same values, and we looked at things the same way. That put it all together for me.

Even after we got married, Janice didn't go to many of our games in Tampa. It wasn't important to her. In fact, she didn't really like going. I remember she would always tell me how the other players' wives wanted to gossip all the time. She would ask me, "Why are so many other people worried about what you're doing?" Everything they said was "Doug's doing this" or they'd be talking about some other player. That's what the wives were involved in.

Janice became real close friends with Jimmy Giles' wife, Vivian. Those two spent a lot of time together. They were two of a kind. Viv didn't get caught up in the gossip, either. She had a son, little Jimmy, and that was her most important thing, taking care of that little boy. Janice and Viv would talk about children and other things that concerned them. They didn't care about football.

I remember how much Janice wanted to have a baby and how excited she was when she found out she was pregnant. She never did go to work after she came to Tampa, because she got pregnant right after we got married. She was happy to stay at home being my wife and becoming a mother. She didn't have an ego problem where she had to be out showing off with all her friends. She was content being my wife. That was enough for her. Then on January 14, 1983, Ashley Monique was born. I was there when Janice delivered the baby. It was fascinating to me, and a wonderful event in my life.

Having Ashley was the greatest thrill in Janice's life. Ashley was always No. 1 with Janice. There was no question about that. When I would come home, Janice would be holding that baby and rocking her. She called her Miss Ashley. It didn't matter to Janice if I was there or not. At that time, Ashley meant the world to her. I didn't mind, because I knew how important that baby was to her. How could I be selfish about it?

Janice had to do almost everything for the baby, because I wasn't very good at it. I guess you could say I'm kind of nervous about handling babies. I'm afraid I might fumble them. Once Ashley got a little older, I enjoyed her a lot more. I liked it when she started to talk, because then she could tell me what she wanted, what she liked and what she didn't like. I enjoyed watching her personality develop.

Ashley was so important to me because I was her father and I had dreams for her. I understood why my parents wanted me to do something with myself. I was so proud of Ashley, and I was happy that she made Janice so happy.

Everything was going great for us. We were really on the upswing in our lives. I was just starting to negotiate my new contract with the Buccaneers, and I was certain they were going to take care of me financially. I finally had Janice as my wife, and we had Ashley. What more could we want? Two little country hicks, who never had much in life, had a chance to make some money and to have a great life together.

9

Making of the Bucs

My first experience with Hugh Culverhouse tipped me off to what was in store for me in Tampa. The Buccaneers picked me in the first round of the 1978 NFL draft. Since they had the worst record in the league the year before, they had the No. 1 pick in the draft. Instead of using it on me, they traded down to No. 17 and drafted me there. I was still the first quarterback picked. I was also the only black quarterback in the league. I had to hold out to get a $50,000 salary for my rookie season. My total package for five years, including a signing bonus, was worth $565,000. A lot of the other first-round picks were getting almost $1 million for the same length of time.

Eight years later, Vinny Testaverde received $8 million from the Bucs for the same length contract. At the time I was negotiating my contract, Phil Krueger, the Bucs general manager, told me it didn't matter what I got paid initially because I wasn't going to play for three or four years anyway. They started out trying to get me to sign for $350,000 for five years. I think they wanted a slave, not a quarterback. So I sat out the first week of training camp until they raised their offer. That was just the beginning of my troubles.

Walking on the field at the Bucs training camp that first day, I could feel the eyes cutting through me. There were a lot of people angry that they drafted me, and the rest were pissed off that I held out for a week. There were fans standing around the gates of the complex, and they just glared at me. I'm sure they thought, "Who does this guy think he is holding out? He should feel lucky to have a chance to play here." The media was watching every step I took. I could hear those damn Japanese cameras clicking every time I moved.

It was already a tough day for me before practice ever started. Then it got worse. I messed up one play, and Bill Nelson, our quarterback coach, jumped all over me. If I hadn't had the home training and Southern mentality of being black, I couldn't have handled it. But I thought, "That's my coach. I've got to take it." Nowadays, if Bill Nelson had pulled that crap on me like he did there, I would have slapped the shit out of him. I felt at the time that I had to respect him. But he didn't respect me as a man.

Joe Gibbs, the Bucs running back coach and offensive coordinator, was at the other end of the complex when it happened. As far away as that, he could still hear Nelson screaming at me. Coach Gibbs came running all the way down the field to stop it.

"Hey, he's got to learn like anyone else," Coach Gibbs shouted, showing his distress with Nelson. "Don't be hollering at him. Give him a chance. He just got here."

Later that day, some people on the team told me that Coach Gibbs and Coach Nelson almost came to blows in the coaches meeting. I appreciated what Coach Gibbs had done. But I realized that would not be the last of it.

The only reason the Bucs drafted me in the first place was they had been so bad. They were willing to do anything to win. It isn't that they wanted a black quarterback. I know Hugh Culverhouse and Phil Krueger didn't want a black quarterback. They told me I wasn't going to play. I found out later that Coach Gibbs and Ken Herock, who is now the Player Personnel Director for the Atlanta Falcons, had to talk them into drafting me. But this is a team that had set the NFL record for losing the most consecutive games. They went 0-26 before finally winning a couple of games at the end of the 1977 season. But that was two wins in two years. They needed to win, and I guess I was their best chance, black or not.

In the preseason, my competition was Mike Boryla and Gary Huff. I knew I could be the starter, and I eventually won the job for the season opener with the New York Giants. Just being named a starter in the NFL was a thrill. It made my season. I wanted to win, but starting as a rookie was really important to me, especially after they told me that I wasn't going to play for three years. I was the No. 1 pick, and I wanted to be the No. 1 quarterback. Hey, I wanted to play.

On opening day we played the New York Giants in Tampa Stadium. It didn't take long for me to sustain my first NFL injury. Gary Jeter hit me out of bounds and I hurt my shoulder. I thought it might have been separated, but I didn't want to come out of the game. Even though I was in a lot of pain, I went back to the huddle and called the next play. I walked up to the line, put my hands under the center, and when I raised my hands, the pain just shot through my arm. It was so bad that I went down to my knees. There were a lot of oohs and aahs from the crowd. Nobody knew what had happened to me. Coach McKay told me later that he thought, "Oh my goodness, they shot him."

After that, I had to come out of the game and ended up missing the next game, too. We lost those first two games, but I came back the third week, and we started playing real well. We won three of our next four games, and people were starting to take notice. That was more games than they had won in the history of the franchise. A lot of people in Tampa were getting excited about the Bucs. But there were still some fans who booed me whenever they got a chance. And I got hate mail.

Whenever I got a letter without a return address, I could be sure it was a nasty letter. Then one day, I got a big package in the mail, and when I opened it, there was a rotten watermelon in it and a note that said, "Try throwing this to your niggers. Maybe they can catch this." I guess they didn't think we had very good receivers.

Coach McKay took a lot of flack for playing me and some of the other black guys. I remember one game we were walking off the field and one of the rednecks in the crowd yelled, "Hey, McKay, why don't you go back to Southern Cal and take your niggers with you." Mac got really mad. He wanted to go up in the stands to discuss the matter. He took a lot of abuse like that.

I always got along great with Coach McKay. He was a dictator on the field, but one on one, he was a fair man. You could go talk to him about anything. It's funny how different he was with just you in the room. He could be pretty tough on the team. Wayne Fontes, now the head coach of the Detroit Lions, was our defensive backfield coach, and Coach McKay used him as his go-between. If Coach wanted something done, he sent Wayne to do it. Wayne would come into our meetings and say, "OK, guys, Coach is coming." Everyone would get real quiet and wait for him.

One game, Coach McKay was mad at the offensive line. He walked into the locker room and said, "You offensive linemen couldn't knock a sick whore off a piss pot." Then he turned around and walked right back out.

Another time we were all playing badly, and he came into the locker room and told us, "You guys are playing like you don't want to be here. Dammit, if you don't want to be here, come see me. I'll trade your ass."

But the real John McKay wasn't like that at all. If you went to his office and needed to talk about something, he was always willing to see you. We would sit down and talk things out. He always seemed to be able to work things out. I still call him to talk. I called him after we won the Super Bowl, and he was really happy for me.

It disturbed Coach McKay that some of the redneck fans mistreated the black players on the team. But that was one problem he couldn't solve. It's evident that Florida is one of the most racist states in the country. I would make the statement to my teammates, "You can't go no farther south than Florida." A lot of people there could not accept that a black man was running their football team. That isn't supposed to happen in America. There hadn't been any black presidents. No governors were black. There weren't many black Congressmen. So here was a black guy who was in complete control of the Tampa Bay Bucs. That just didn't sit right with a lot of folks.

There were some people in the area who didn't see color. One of them was Buddy Foster, who I'm still good friends with. I drove a demo for his car dealership, and he always invited me over to his house. In fact, he gave me a going away party when I left the team.

We were having a good season in 1978, and everything seemed to be headed in the right direction for me and the Bucs. Our first big game came against the Chicago Bears. There was a sellout crowd in Tampa Stadium, and I threw two touchdown passes. One was to Morris Owens, and the other was to Jim Obradovich, the tight end. We won the game, 33-19. That made us 4-4, and we were in the race for the Central Division title.

Tampa was really fired up over the team. We had come a long way, and we had a good chance to win the division and make the playoffs. I wanted to be a part of it. I wanted to be a leader of the team. Everything seemed great. Most of the fans seemed great. The organization seemed great. But I was naive at the time.

I was getting paid, not a lot, but I was still getting paid. My way of thinking was I signed a contract to play, and I was going to fulfill my contract. I believed they would take care of me. At the time, I didn't really care about money. We were in the thick of the race, and I felt great. I thought this was going to be my team for as long as I played in the NFL.

From my standpoint, the season ended the next week. We were playing the Los Angeles Rams in the Coliseum, and I got hurt bad. I ran into my man who plays Hunter on the television series. I still like Fred Dryer and watch his show all the time, even if he did bust me up in the second quarter. It was just a regular play. I went back to pass and completed a sideline route to Jimmy Giles for about fifteen yards. Immediately after I threw the ball, I received a ferocious hit. It was a clean hit. But man, it was hard. Dryer smashed into my helmet with such force that the side of the helmet was pushed into my jaw and crushed it. I never would look at that play on film.

When I went down, there wasn't a lot of pain. I just ran my tongue around my teeth and knew something was wrong. I thought Dryer had just knocked some teeth loose. It felt real loose on the left side of my jaw, but it seemed like it was just my teeth. That's what I told our dentist when he came out to look at me. He told me to come to the sideline so he could look at it some more. After a little while, he said, "No, I think it's more than teeth, Doug. You've got a broken jaw."

As we walked to the dressing room, I couldn't believe this was happening. We were in this big game, and I needed to be out there. The dentist gave me some pain medicine and just wrapped my whole head up to keep me from opening my mouth. The game was scoreless when I left, but the Rams went on to win 26-23. It was a real letdown because it was a game we could have won. It would have given us a winning record, and we could taste a championship. I had to ride home on the team plane with my head still wrapped up. It was a five-hour flight. They did the oral surgery that night.

My mouth was wired up for six weeks. All I could eat was milk-shakes. You can't imagine how sick you can get of milkshakes. I would get cravings for some real food. My mom came to visit me, and I wanted some red beans so bad. She cooked me some red beans, rice and smoked sausage. I put it in a blender, mixed it up and drank it. I just wanted the taste. I had to have it. Still, I lost 20 pounds and was down to 195.

Everything fell apart for the Bucs during those six weeks. Mike Rae, who came over to us from the Raiders, took my place. We lost six out of seven games. The only one we won was against Buffalo. I came back for the last game of the year. Even though we were 5-10 and out of the race, we still had 55,000 people in the stadium to watch us play the New Orleans Saints. That shows the interest there was in the team.

The Saints killed us, and we finished 5-11. But it was still an exciting year, and it gave a preview of what was to come. If I hadn't gotten hurt, we probably would have won more games. I don't know if we would have won the division, but I think we would have won more than five games.

In games that I started, we were 4-4, which showed I could be successful in the league, even as a rookie. I was a unanimous choice for NFL All-Rookie quarterback, had been picked NFC Player of the Week in our win over Kansas City and had my first 300-yard game in a win over Minnesota. It was a good start, but I was hungry for more.

The next year was ours. We had a bunch of guys who were tired of getting their brains beat out. They felt they had an opportunity to make something happen. We had a theme song, "Ain't No Stoppin' Us Now." We played that record over and over again in the dressing room. We played it every day in training camp. We played it every day during the season. And we believed it.

Before we knew it, we were 5-0 and rolling again. The game that I remember most was the fifth one. We had fallen behind to the Bears in Chicago, but we put together a great drive toward the end of the game. I hit Issac Hagins in the corner of the end zone for a touchdown, and we won 17-13.

Our confidence level was sky high. We were the only undefeated team left in the NFL, and we didn't think we could be beat. We kept playing "Ain't No Stoppin' Us Now," and it really seemed like that.

Then we went to Giants Stadium, and the Giants brought us back to earth. It was a close game, but we ended up losing 17-14. Our morale was still high, yet we realized that no team is unbeatable. The biggest thing about the game was our best running back, Jimmy DuBose, got hurt, and I thought it was my fault. I threw a pass, it was tipped, and the Giants intercepted it. Jimmy hurt his knee trying to make the tackle. I blamed myself for it, because I threw the pass. It really hurt the team, because Jimmy was running real well at the time. Without him, our game plan was out of whack.

We still had some good wins and got to 9-3, but then we had the slump. We lost three in a row, and it almost cost us the championship. The low point came against San Francisco when I threw six interceptions, and we lost 23-7. I just couldn't get anything going. It was like everything was in slow motion, and I had no emotion. I was so lethargic. We were just out there. We thought we were going to win easily, because San Francisco wasn't winning. We thought we were just going to run over them. We did everything in the world to help them win, especially me with all those interceptions.

Just before that, we had played Minnesota and made one hell of a comeback. I remember scrambling all around, diving in the corner of the end zone for the TD and almost breaking my ass. Then we had the extra point blocked, and they beat us 23-22. That day, we had a field goal and an extra point blocked. But that's what happens in a slump.

That's when the press really got on me, and our fans were howling. They said I had taken the team as far as I could, and we needed another quarterback.

The last week of the season, we were faced with elimination. If we beat Kansas City, we would win the division title and go to the playoffs. But if we lost, Chicago would be the division champion and our season would be over. There was a driving rain storm in Tampa that day. Nobody had scored going into the final minutes of the game, and it was make or break. We put together a nice drive, and Neil O'Donoghue came in to attempt a 19-yard field goal. Neil hit the field goal and we beat the Chiefs to move into the playoffs.

Winning the division championship was an unbelievable feeling.

You couldn't find a way to describe the feeling of going from the bottom of your division to winning it. That was one heck of a time for us. Minnesota had been dominating the Central Division at that time, and all of a sudden, you've got a new kid on the block who wins it all. The Bucs had been in existence for only four years, and we were the champions. It was the earliest in NFL history that an expansion team had won a division title. I became the only quarterback in the NFL to make it to a conference championship game in my first two years in the league. I was just glad to be part of something like that. It put a great closeness on the team. We were a young team, and we thought we were going to go a long way.

Our first playoff game was with the Philadelphia Eagles. This was a team with known stars like Ron Jaworski, Wilbert Montgomery and Harold Carmichael. A lot of people thought they were going to be a Super Bowl team, and they eventually made it two years later. We just had a bunch of no-names, and they were expected to beat us easily. They were favored by a touchdown or more.

I remember throwing two touchdown passes to Jimmy Giles. We were playing at home, and the stadium was going crazy. It was a sea of orange. That was some kind of game. We ended up winning 24-17.

All of a sudden, we were in the NFC championship game. The only thing between us and the Super Bowl was the Los Angeles Rams. I mean we were on the verge of going from the worst team in pro sports to the Super Bowl in a matter of two years. It was a great feeling.

From a personal standpoint, I can't say how much I had to do with our success. That isn't for me to say. I know I played an integral part in it, not only as a quarterback, but as a leader. I think I was able to make the other guys on the team believe in me and believe in themselves. That was very satisfying to me.

During the week of the championship game, it seemed like some people on the team were already looking ahead to the Super Bowl. I know the fans were. We had already beaten the Rams earlier that year, 21-6. We had them in Tampa Stadium, and I think we were overconfident.

I don't even think the coaching staff prepared as well as it had in other games that season. Our game plan stunk up the place. I hate to even think about some of the things we did. All we tried to do was pitch right, pitch left, and keep running Ricky Bell. We didn't have any imagination that day. I don't even know who the offensive coordinator was. I really don't. Coach Gibbs was gone. I don't think we had a legitimate offensive coordinator. Bill Nelson was the quarterback coach. Coach McKay called the plays.

The game ended early for me. I got hurt in the third quarter. Mike Fanning of the Rams came across my right arm and tore my bicep. I think the worst thing that I did was to come out in street clothes after I got hurt. That team believed in Doug Williams. I think they thought, "If we can keep it close, then Doug will find a way to win." But when I came out in street clothes, it killed any hope that we had. We never did score, and the Rams won 9-0.

Losing the championship game was disappointing, because we really believed we were going to win. But I think what showed in that game was playoff experience. The Rams had been there, and we had not. One thing I have found out about the NFL is there are two seasons. There's the regular season, and there's the playoffs. I learned that best with the Redskins. They are a totally different team at playoff time. That was the problem with the Bucs. We didn't have any playoff experience, whereas the Rams had been in that situation. We were still enjoying the experience of being in the playoffs. They turned it up a notch, and we stayed at that same level. If we had been prepared for that game, instead of looking at two weeks in Anaheim for the Super Bowl, we would have been all right. You can't expect to win like that.

Even though we lost that game to the Rams, it was one heck of a season for us. Here is this expansion team that had been 0-26 in its second season, and two years later, we were the last undefeated team in the NFL at 5-0, we won the Central Division championship, we won our first playoff game, and we played for the conference title. Everyone on the team was proud of our accomplishments. The fans were behind us. Tampa Stadium was always sold out. All that anyone wanted to talk about was the Bucs. The whole city kept talking about "Worst to First." That was our theme.

What was most important to me was being the leader of the team. I knew what I could do on the field. Some people might have looked at my stats and said it wasn't all that good of a year. I threw for 2,448 yards and 18 touchdowns. But a lot of people just wanted to talk about my completion rate of 41.8. But I also set an NFL record by being sacked only 7 times in 404 pass attempts.

Stats are for losers. There are a lot of quarterbacks in the league who complete 60 percent of their passes and never play on a winning team, much less a championship team. What's better, completing three passes for nine yards and having fourth-and-one or completing one out of three and getting twenty yards on the play? We didn't have a great offensive line, so I had to throw the ball away sometimes when I would have been sacked. I was trying to help the team, not help Doug Williams' stats. Make the plays, damn the stats. When I look at quarterbacks who take sacks to keep their stats in order, it really makes me mad. I don't play like that.

By that time, I felt there was nothing that any other quarterback in the league could do that I couldn't do. I had never had any problems with the NFL game. Football is football to me, and that's the way I always looked at it. When you leave high school to go to college, you turn it up a notch. When you leave college to the pros, you turn it up another notch. I thought I had done everything I could for the Bucs in 1979, and I think my teammates felt the same way.

After that season, some guys on the team wanted to renegotiate their contracts. I had been paid $60,000 that season as the quarterback of a division champion. I knew the other quarterbacks in the league were making $200,000 or $300,000. But I never thought about asking for more. I had signed a contract and I was going to live up to it. I always believed that being loyal was the most important thing. I honestly believed the Bucs would take care of me when the time came. I had three years left on my contract, and I was going to fulfill it and do everything I could to get us back into the playoffs.

The 1980 season started off with such high expectations. They got even higher when we beat Cincinnati and then the Rams in our first two games. It was a revenge type of game against the Rams. We beat them 10-9 and we really thought that this was a big step forward for us. But after that, we just couldn't get a handle on anything. It turned into a terrible year after that. We won only three more games all season.

Statistically, I had my best game and best season in 1980. I threw for 486 yards, the fourth-highest total in NFL history at the time, and four touchdowns against Minnesota, but the Vikings won 38-30. For the season, I threw for 3,396 yards and 20 touchdowns. Those are good statistics, but they don't mean anything when you lose. That's why I don't think stats are indicative of how well someone has played.

We made so many mistakes that year. Those things happen in pro sports. Look at the Redskins. After we won the Super Bowl in 1988, we went 7-9 the next season. That can happen to any team. You have to realize that people are going to come after you and they want to win just as badly as you do.

Another factor in 1980 was personal problems on the team. It was evident we had some people who had drug problems. But that wasn't our only problem, and I think it was a cheap shot by Hugh Culverhouse to say drugs was the downfall of the Bucs. That wasn't true. There was only one player who was publicly named. There were probably three or four other guys who had drug problems. They were key players, but I still don't think it was fair to blame them for the bad year.

I didn't know too much about what was going on with the drug situation, because I didn't go to the parties and wasn't involved in those types of things. I would liked to have done something to help the guys. But it wasn't like they wanted other people to know what they were doing. If you went to them, it would have been denial, denial, denial. They did it in private.

Another thing that affected the team was some of the guys wanted to renegotiate. That's when management turned a deaf ear to the players. Culverhouse was interested in one thing, and that was making money. I don't even think he cared about winning. I know he didn't care about his players. We were pieces of meat to him.

At the same time, we were still a young team and made a lot of mistakes that year. And we were still the same old team when it came to imagination. We didn't have any. Run, run and throw on third-and-long.

We had been winning on emotion, and emotions will carry you only so far. If we had had a little more talent, to go along with our emotion, we would have been in the Super Bowl.

It was tough to slip back like we did. We were looking forward to being back in the playoffs and making another run at it. We just didn't do the things we needed to do to get there.

In order to have a successful season, you have to go into the year with a clean slate. All the players have to take care of their personal problems. You need support from management. And you need coaches who have a good attitude and plan about how to defeat opponents.

The only time the Bucs' coaching staff prepared for an opponent was the week before we played them. Our coaches played golf all summer. I don't really blame Coach McKay. At Washington, the coaches spend the whole offseason trying to put together a game plan for the opponents. That really makes a difference when it comes time to play them.

After that losing season, our backs were against the wall. We had done so much, so early, that it would have been devastating to just drop right out of it. The 1981 season was critical for us.

It was the type of year that we had to fight hard to keep our heads above water. We would win one, then we would lose one. Detroit had a good team that year, and it was a battle to keep up with the Lions. Going into the final game of the season, we were 8-7 and had pulled dead even with the Lions, but we had to play Detroit in the season finale.

The tie-breaker game was in the Silverdome, and the Lions were undefeated at home that season. That was one of the toughest places in the league to play, because it could get so loud when the Lions were playing well. Our job was to try to take the fans out of the game.

Just before halftime, Kevin House went deep, and I threw the ball about sixty yards. He just outran his guy, caught the ball and went all the way for an eighty-four-yard touchdown. I remember the Silverdome was so quiet you could hear a church mouse. That put us ahead 17-7 at halftime, and we were in good shape. The fans never got started again, and we went on to win 20-17 and earn our second Central Division championship in three years.

We were back in the playoffs, and there was more talk about a Super Bowl. But we had to play at Dallas in our first playoff game. I remember when we came out for pregame warmups in Texas Stadium, one of our offensive tackles, Charlie Hannah, couldn't take his eyes off Ed "Too Tall" Jones. I could hear him saying, "Man, look how big Too Tall is." Well, Charlie was supposed to block Too Tall that day. It seemed like Too Tall and Harvey Martin had a plan to meet up in our backfield every play. The Cowboys shellacked us 38-0.

Still, we had won another division title and returned to the playoffs. I had put together another good year, throwing for 3,563 yards and 19 touchdowns and completing over 50 percent for the first time. I was voted the team's Most Valuable Player by the media for the second straight year. We were a young team with a bright future. Everyone thought we would have a lot more years together and eventually win the Super Bowl.

So many things were happening to me in 1982. Janice and I got married in April. Then it wasn't long before she got pregnant. It was also the last year of my contract, and everyone wanted to talk about that. Then there was the threat of a players strike.

At the time, I was against the strike. The union wanted to get 55 percent of the profits. That didn't really matter to me. I was on the last year of my contract, and the most important thing to me was being able to negotiate a long-term contract. I had to be concerned about free agency, and that's what I wanted them to fight for. I was totally against striking for a percentage of the profits. So when they had the handshakes at midfield, I never did go out.

Right before the strike started, we were playing the Washington Redskins in the second game of the season, and we fumbled the snap from center four times. Everybody suspected that the snap didn't come up, because I was against the strike. I personally didn't think our center, Steve Wilson, would do something like that. It was raining real hard, and the ball was wet. I believe that's why we fumbled so much, not because Steve was trying to make me look bad.

The strike lasted eight weeks, and it was even tougher on us because we had lost our first two games. I had to do something to keep my mind off the strike, so I played golf every day with Jimmy Giles. We played all over the area. We had a good friend Rick Rickette who owned a furniture store. He liked golf and went with us all the time. I never did get very good at it. I guess I had too much on my mind. It's hard to concentrate when you don't have a job.

Janice really helped me during that time. She was always willing to listen to my problems and was very supportive of what I wanted to do. It was a frustrating time for me, but she helped console me. We would go watch movies and just do different things together. Plus, she wasn't a big spender so I didn't have to worry about all the money going out and nothing coming in.

When they finally settled the strike, it was very satisfying to me the way we came back as a team. We lost to Dallas to fall to 0-3, but then we started winning again and before long we were right back in the playoff picture. The big thing was how we were winning. We had so many great comebacks.

The one that really stands out was against the Chicago Bears in the last game of the season. We had to come from behind to get into overtime. I threw for 367 yards and two touchdowns, both to Jimmy Giles, in the second half, and we ended up winning 26-23. With that, we finished with five victories in our final six games. Earlier, we had a good comeback against Detroit, which had another good team. We were down 21-10 but rallied to win 23-21. Another big win for us was a 23-17 victory over the Miami Dolphins on Monday night.

It could have been a disastrous season, but we had turned it into another winning year. We finished 5-4 and qualified for the playoffs. The way we came back so many times showed that our team wasn't going to quit.

In the playoffs, we were glad to get another shot at Dallas, even though the Cowboys had another good team that year. We felt the 1981 game didn't show what we were capable of doing, and we really wanted to play them again. We were having a good game against them. In fact, we were leading in the second half. But then things started to change. I think what turned the game in the Cowboys' favor were two bad calls by the officials. First they called a holding penalty against us and then they called a clipping penalty. That left us with third down and about thirty-five yards to go. I tried to throw the ball deep, but it was intercepted, and they came down to score. That took the momentum away from us, and the Cowboys went on to win, 30-17.

Losing to the Cowboys again was a disappointment, but at least we made progress. We were getting closer. We were starting to get the experience we needed to beat a team like that. Remember this was still only the seventh year of the franchise and my fifth season. We had made the playoffs three out of the last four years. We had two division championships. It looked like there were some great years ahead.

I didn't expect to have any trouble working out a contract with the Bucs. Not once had I ever asked for more money. In 1982, I was paid $120,000. That was the fifty-fourth highest salary for NFL quarterbacks. I mean everybody's backup was making more than me. But I really believed the Bucs were going to give me the kind of money I deserved and we could start getting ready for 1983. I didn't think it would be any trouble at all.

What more could I ask for? I now had a wonderful wife, a beautiful little baby and a promising team to play for. Finally, I was going to be earning the same kind of money that everyone else in the league was getting. But more importantly, I thought I was on a team headed to the top. I wanted to win in the NFL, and I wanted to do it in Tampa.

10

Breaking of the Bucs

In my mind I deserved a good contract after playing for peanuts those first five years. I think most people in Tampa thought I would get rewarded for what I had done for the Bucs. Remember where they had been before I got there, and how far they had come in five years. We felt the success was certain to continue and we would soon have a chance to play in a Super Bowl.

I won for the Bucs, and I represented them with dignity. I had lived up to my commitment. And when it came time to sign a new deal, I didn't think it would be a problem. But I was naive.

First of all, I never should have been a free agent in 1983. The Bucs should have given me a new contract the year before, and I never would have become a free agent.

The Bucs made their qualifying offer in February, and then my agent Jimmy Walsh began to negotiate with Phil Krueger, the general manager. Hugh Culverhouse refused to deal with Jimmy, so he had to negotiate with Krueger. We asked for a five-year contract for $600,000 a year. Their best offer was $400,000 a year. Krueger said if they went any higher, it would upset the salary scale on the team and everyone else would want more money.

But we weren't talking about everyone else. I wasn't going to be their slave anymore. I wanted what I was worth. It was hard for me to believe that they wouldn't sign me. I knew my teammates couldn't believe it. I think they were more upset than I was about it. You're talking about the leader of that football team. I think the other guys felt if they treat Doug Williams that way, they probably don't give a damn about me, either.

Culverhouse wanted me to sign another cut-rate deal. And he used some underhanded tactics to try to lure me into it. He tried to intimidate me through the press, and then he tried to do it in person. He's from Alabama, went to school at the University of Alabama and got his law degree there. When it comes down to it, he's just a redneck from Alabama. He made his money as a tax attorney. He had plenty of money, but he wanted to make sure nobody got any of it.

One day, Culverhouse called me into his office and said he wanted to sign a contract with me and offer me a piece of a real estate deal that would make me secure for the rest of my life. He told me to sign a line of credit for $250,000 to put into the real estate deal. He said we would make millions of dollars off it.

"Mr. Culverhouse, I don't know anything about real estate. I don't think I can sign this," I told him.

I didn't have any money because he hadn't given me a contract yet. What he was trying to do was make me sign a note, and then I'd be $250,000 in debt and I'd have to sign any contract he offered me. I wasn't dumb enough to let him suck me into it. Some guys would have thought about those millions of dollars he said we'd make and figure it was a good deal. But I knew if I signed that note, he would have me right where he wanted me. It was one of his good ol' buddy deals. He didn't want my agent involved. It was going to be some kind of office building and shopping center on Dale Mabry Boulevard in Tampa.

Culverhouse told me in that Southern redneck drawl of his: "I'm tryin' to give you a deel so you'll be financially seecure for the rest of your life, buddy."

I wanted to tell him, "Go to hell with your 'deel,' Culverhouse." But he was the team owner, and I couldn't tell him that his "deel" stunk. Later on, he sent me a certified letter, and all I had to do was sign it and I'd have the line of credit.

Culverhouse thought that I was a good ol' black boy who never had nothin' and would go along with whatever Mr. Culverhouse wanted. He paid me like a slave, but I wasn't that much of a slave to sign that deal. That real estate project went belly up. They never did break ground on it.

If I had signed that line of credit, Culverhouse would have had me right where he wanted me. I would have needed the money from the contract, so I would have had to sign for anything he offered me. Who was going to pay the bills? I didn't have $250,000 to put into something like that. I wasn't going to be his sucker. It just shows the type of mentality Culverhouse had. He thought I would jump at anything and be glad to have it.

My honest impression of Hugh Culverhouse is pretty much the same as everybody who knows him. If someone wanted a perfect redneck asshole, Culverhouse would be a top candidate. He would always come up to you and say, "Haw's the fam-lee?" And you could tell he didn't mean it. He took football strictly as a business. He looked at his players as pieces of meat. Just talent. Write 'em off, let 'em go. We all knew what kind of person we were dealing with.

I remember how his wife, Joy, would come to training camp when it was so hot and she would sit in a chair at the back of the complex and hold her umbrella up over her head. She would just sit and stare at her boys. Then after a while she would get up and leave. We used to tease each other about being the Culverhouses' boys.

Now it was different with Coach McKay. I always thought John McKay was a fair man. If it had been up to him, I would have got my money from the Bucs. I remember one time he called me into his office to talk about the contract.

"Dougie, just take it easy," he said reassuringly. "You're going to get your money. I'm a firm believer that blacks are the best athletes. You deserve the money."

Mac was always fair. He recognized the value of blacks and treated us right. Look at his teams at Southern Cal. He had a lot of blacks and they won national championships. Coach McKay wanted me to get my money, but his hands were tied. He was still working for Culverhouse, and basically, he had to go along with whatever Culverhouse wanted.

About the time my contract talks bogged down, Janice started to get these headaches. But she was the type of person who would just say, "Don't worry about me, I'll take something for it, and then I'll be all right."

It was Easter time, and we decided to drive home to Louisiana for the holiday. One morning while we were there, Janice woke up with a terrible headache. We took her out to a doctor in Zachary. He examined her and could see there was a problem. So he sent us to Baton Rouge to a specialist, Dr. Poche. He ordered a CAT scan, and it showed a brain tumor.

Dr. Poche came into the hospital room and talked to us together. He said the tumor was large, about the size of a grapefruit. Then he explained the situation. We had to make a decision about surgery, because the tumor could burst at any moment and cause instant death.

I remember looking at her, and she started crying. She said, "What will happen to my baby?"

"Ashley is going to be all right, Janice," I said, trying to comfort her. "You know I'm going to take care of her. Now we've got to make a decision."

"Whatever we've got to do, Doug," she answered. "Let's have the operation."

The surgery was scheduled the next morning at Our Lady of the Lake Regional Medical Center. It was a long operation, but they thought it was successful. She seemed to come out of it pretty well, and then she got stronger and stronger through the week. It really seemed like she was going to be well again.

One week later, she was still in the hospital, and that day she called my Daddy and, later, a couple of her friends. It was so good to see her remembering things and talking to people. I was really encouraged.

Then that night, it was storming outside, and she started screaming again. The headache had come back, and she couldn't keep any fluids down. She was in tremendous pain. I tried to console her, but it didn't help, so we had to call the doctor. They ordered us out of the room. While they were trying to help her, fluid built up in her chest. Finally, her lungs collapsed, and she died.

At that time, my life just stopped. It was one of those stages where no matter what you've accomplished in life, no matter what you have, it doesn't matter. If I could have given up my football career to save Janice, I would have. If I could have given up my right arm, my left arm, every nickel and dime I had, I would have. I would have given anything to save her, but I couldn't. I was willing to sacrifice anything I had, but you just don't make those kind of deals.

Losing Janice was the toughest thing I have ever been through. I can't imagine anything being worse, except maybe if something happened to Ashley. I had never faced anything like it. I had never lost anyone I cared that much about. I think I have been able to use Janice's death to help myself overcome other things, because nothing could be more difficult to bear than that. You don't ever get over it. Even today when I look at Ashley, I think of Janice. They look so much alike. To be honest, I'm glad they do, because I don't ever want to forget Janice.

Football didn't mean anything to me after Janice died. It didn't matter to me if I ever played again. All I cared about was taking care of Ashley. I was willing to become a high school coach, live at home in Zachary, and then Ashley and I would live happily ever after. It didn't matter what I had to give up, I wanted to be there for her.

I remember how M'Dear came through for me, like she always has. She told me, "Doug, don't you worry about that baby. I'll take care of her." She quit her job and took Ashley in just like she was her own child. I wanted Ashley to grow up in Zachary, because it's a great place to raise a child. It was such a relief to know that Ashley was going to be with my mom.

Even though I didn't really care what the Bucs were going to offer me, it was still a matter of principle. I had been through enough. I couldn't take anything else tearing me down, and what the Bucs were trying to do was a slap in the face. To me, they were saying, "Doug Williams, you're not worth what other quarterbacks are worth." I couldn't take that.

Then at Janice's funeral, I remember Culverhouse showing up, and it was so much like a Mafia movie. They came there in one of those long black limousines, and as soon as it was over, they got right back in their limo and drove out of there. I mean they got out of there as quickly as they could. They never said anything to me. They showed no sympathy. It was obvious they weren't concerned.

From a public standpoint, they just wanted to show that they were there at Doug Williams' wife's funeral. It was all a ploy. They probably called the newspaper to tell them what they had just done. Jimmy Giles and I talked a lot about that, how they came and left in such a hurry.

I think Culverhouse was playing on my weakness. He thought

since I had lost my wife, it would be easy pickings to sign this guy. He's all distraught and upset about her death. He has a daughter to take care of. At that point, the Bucs thought I would take anything. But hey, I wasn't going to play for peanuts. They needed to make a real commitment to me, or I was going to kiss football goodbye. I really didn't care at that point. Football wasn't that important anymore.

Soon after that, Bill Tatham called me about playing for his team, the Oklahoma Outlaws. I wasn't really interested in the USFL, but Tatham caught my attention. He seemed really concerned about me. Right away, I could tell he was so different than Culverhouse. He showed me some respect and treated me like I mattered to him. He was willing to give me the $3 million, five-year contract that I wanted. He told me to call if I was interested in playing for him. I thought about it for a while, but I wasn't sure I wanted to move to Oklahoma.

I had already moved home to Zachary, and my mom was taking care of Ashley. I was substitute teaching at Northwestern Middle School and planning to go into coaching the next year. I was ready to get on with my life away from pro football.

But the Bucs still wanted to sign me. The exhibition season was just starting when I heard from them again. I remember it was the day of the Hall of Fame game. I got a call from Ken Herock, their director of player personnel, and he asked if I could come to Tampa that day. I couldn't come right then, because my Daddy was in the hospital and had to have his leg amputated. There was no way I would miss being with him. But I told Ken that I would come the next day.

What I expected was for the Bucs to raise their offer. I figured they were tired of waiting and were going to pay me what I wanted. But that wasn't the case at all.

First, I was told to go see Coach McKay. He was really glad to see me and we talked for a while. Then he told me, "Dougie, I think that you should take what they're offering. I don't think the old man is going to go higher than $400,000."

"Coach, I can't sign for that," I told him. "I won't accept that. I can't play for that."

Well, I could tell Coach McKay was disappointed. He told me to go see Phil Krueger, that maybe he could work something out.

When I went in to see Krueger, he started talking about how much season ticket sales had gone down because I hadn't signed.

Then he said Culverhouse told him they could only afford to pay me $375,000.

"Phil, it's not my job to sell tickets," I said, cutting him off. "You didn't tell me my contract was based on ticket sales. Maybe I should have asked for more. How many sellouts have we had?"

By then, I was really mad, and he could tell it. So he backed off and said he could give me the $400,000 salary and throw in some incentives. If I threw so many touchdown passes, I would get this much. If I finished in the top eight quarterbacks, I would get that much. If I did such and such, I would get so much more. It all added up to $75,000 of incentives.

"Phil, first of all, I came here and you said I wasn't going to play for three years and I signed a contract based on that," I told him. "Now you're telling me you'll give me some if-money, if I do this, if I do whatever. You know I've never complained about anything in the five years I've been here. I didn't have the best offensive line in football. I didn't have the best receivers. I never complained. Phil, I don't want none of your if-money. I don't want any. Either pay me what I deserve or I won't play for you."

Krueger said that was the best he could do, so I got up and left his office. I knew it was all over. That was the last time I talked to the Bucs. They told the newspapers that they had offered me $600,000, like I had wanted. They maintain today that they offered me $600,000. But that wasn't true. They never raised their offer over $400,000.

Soon after that, I called my agent, Jimmy Walsh, and told him, "Let's go with Bill Tatham."

Jimmy Walsh had represented Joe Namath and worked in New York. But Jimmy was naive. He used to talk about how much they paid Namath back in the 1960s and 1970s. I told him, "Jimmy, I am not Joe Namath. You've got to realize you're negotiating for Doug Williams: six-foot-four, dark skin, brown eyes. You're not dealing with no blue-eyed boy." I had to tell him what he was dealing with. Nobody was going to pay me what Joe Namath made, no matter how many championships I won. I was smart enough to recognize what was happening. But it took Jimmy awhile to understand it. I don't think Jimmy did the best job representing me. A lot of things got back to me later that Jimmy never told me about. That is one reason why Jimmy no longer represents me. I think both sides messed up during the whole ordeal.

In Tampa, I was made to look like the villain, because the press printed everything the Bucs told them. I couldn't really tell my side of the story, because I knew if I caused too much of a flack, Culverhouse and Krueger would do anything they could to try to hurt me. The owners and general managers in the NFL work so closely together that all it would take is a call from Culverhouse and I might not ever play in the league again. I didn't want to take the chance of being blackballed.

Everything the Bucs did was designed to make sure Doug Williams was buried. Whenever management talked about the team, they never mentioned my name. Doug Williams was completely omitted. They tried to make it seem like I never existed. The only time I remember my name being mentioned again by the Bucs was when Vinny Testaverde was close to breaking my record for most touchdowns in one season. But they didn't say much about Vinny breaking the team record for interceptions with 35. They paid Vinny $8 million, and he threw 35 interceptions. If I had thrown 35 interceptions in one season, they would have hung me up by my toes. But they said Vinny was a promising young quarterback who just needed some time.

In the Bucs' 1982 highlight film, I was taken out of every scene. Whenever there was a long pass, they would only show the receiver catching the ball. They never once showed the quarterback. It's funny because the NFL's highlight film of the Bucs season shows me in a lot of places.

The Bucs' media guide has no mention of my name, other than in the team records and listing of past players. Its rundown of year-by-year highlights doesn't mention me once.

What the Bucs failed to recognize is they weren't just paying for a quarterback. They were paying for leadership. The guys on that team believed in Doug Williams. They believed if there was a way to get it done, Doug would find a way to do it. Some of my teammates told me how upset they were. I'm sure they thought, "If they don't appreciate Doug, they don't appreciate me, either."

The Bucs have paid dearly for letting me get away. They went 2-14 the year I left and the stadium was practically empty. They've had seven straight losing seasons and have never approached the success we had. Attendance has plummeted in Tampa Stadium, where sellout crowds of 68,000-plus were the rule. In our worst year, we drew 55,000 a game.

In 1983, they set a team record with 28,000 no-shows for one game. Two years later, they drew a record-low crowd of 25,777 for another home game. And since then, crowds of less than 30,000 aren't unusual. Culverhouse has threatened to move home games to Orlando. But it's not the fans' fault. He sold the team out. They've lost so many good players—Jimmy Giles and Kevin House left not long after I did.

The Bucs couldn't even sign Bo Jackson. Bo's agent, Richard Woods, called me to find out what I thought about the team. I didn't know his agent, so I was hesitant to talk about it. But he told me that Bo had just visited Tampa and needed more input on the team.

"I don't think it's something that I should tell you," I said guardedly. "I think it's something you should find out on your own."

"Well, Bo didn't feel comfortable down there," Woods told me. "He felt that Culverhouse wasn't being up front, that he was trying to jerk him around. Culverhouse told the media that he wants to make Bo the highest paid player in the league, but that's not what he's doing."

Actually, Culverhouse was offering Bo some kind of off-the-wall deal, like he did with me and that shopping center.

Woods said Bo wanted to know why the Bucs let me get away. Bo thought that showed they weren't willing to do what it takes to win. Bo told his agent, "Culverhouse has some red behind his neck." It was obvious Bo didn't feel comfortable dealing with someone like Culverhouse.

It's good that Bo had the strength to decide where he wanted to play, what he was willing to take, and with whom he was willing to deal.

A big part of the Bucs' downfall is that they've lost so many high draft picks. Bo was a No. 1 pick, and they lost him to baseball. Ron Holmes was a No. 1 pick for the Bucs and he played in the Super Bowl for the Broncos this year. In 1979, they gave up a No. 1 pick to Chicago for Wally Chambers, and the Bears got Dan Hampton, who helped them win a Super Bowl. And of course, I was a No. 1 pick and ended up winning a Super Bowl for another team. They just keep messing everything up.

The main thing I like about the Bucs failing is Culverhouse losing money. The team has lost millions of dollars in gate receipts alone. I never thought Tampa Stadium would be so empty. When it comes to the bottom line, no one wants to watch a loser, even one with a white quarterback.

11

A New League

When I agreed to play in the United States Football League, I was only twenty-seven and in the prime of my career. But I realized the mentality of the Tampa Bay Buccaneers. Hugh Culverhouse was not going to pay a black man what white quarterbacks were making. I guess I shouldn't have expected any more from him. I thought being loyal meant something, but obviously I was wrong. They didn't appreciate me at all. It didn't mean anything to them that I helped turn the Bucs into winners.

From my perspective, playing in the USFL was just an opportunity to continue my football career. I would have played for any team or any league that was willing to pay me what I was worth. And Bill Tatham did that.

Bill Tatham is a good man, and he has always treated me like I was somebody, not just a number. His whole family was good to me. They made me feel welcome. I got along great with Bill, his father Bill, Sr., and his whole family. They made their money in the real estate business. I don't know how much they had, but it was enough to buy a professional football team. They also own part of the Utah Jazz, and they're big boosters of Fresno State. It's obvious they enjoy being involved in sports, and they do that by investing in teams. If I could afford it, I'd love to do the same thing. I'd like to own a football team or a baseball club or any other type of sports team. But I don't have that kind of capital. You're talking about megabucks. You can't buy a team for $5,000 like they did with the old AFL teams. It's more like $100 million.

Now Bill, Jr., was tough when it came to running his team, the Oklahoma Outlaws. But I can understand that. You know what the golden rule is: The man who's got the gold makes the rule. So I accepted that and enjoyed my relationship with the Tathams. They treated me like a man and made me feel like they wanted me to be part of the organization and even part of their family.

I've been told that even today when you walk into the Tatham's home in Fresno, California, there's a picture of Doug Williams right there where you enter the house. That means a lot to me. You're talking about a white family and obviously color doesn't matter to them. That makes me feel good. I'm sure if the Tathams ever bought another professional football franchise, I'd get a call to come work for them. That shows how different their attitude is from Culverhouse and Phil Krueger's. I didn't ask to be treated better than anybody else. All I wanted was to get what everybody else got and to be treated like everybody else.

What I liked best about the USFL was that it created more jobs in professional football. More opportunities for players, more for coaches. Of course, if you looked around the league, there weren't any black coaches and there weren't many black quarterbacks. Reggie Collier, Vince Evans and myself. That was it. So the concept was pretty much the same as far as black quarterbacks. We were still dealing with societal prejudices.

I really liked the city of Tulsa, though it's not a great football town. The Outlaws never drew that many people for our games. Usually we had a crowd of about 15,000. But it's probably the cleanest city that I've ever been in. I think it would be a great place to raise a family, and it was a super place to live. I enjoyed the year I stayed there. The only thing I didn't like was living down the street from Oral Roberts.

There was a lot of talk about how hard it was going to be playing in the spring and summer. But I wasn't going to let the weather affect me. Playing football was my job, and I was willing to play in any kind of weather or at any time of the year. Mentally, you can't let yourself be affected by things like that. Sure, it was tough going to training camp in the spring. That's usually your offseason. But once you get involved in practice and getting ready to play, you realize this is your season and you've got to make the best of it.

I always liked the sun and heat anyway. I just enjoy sweating. I grew up in hot weather, so it wasn't anything new to me. We didn't have that many hot days in Tulsa anyway. It was a real cold spring in 1984, and it seemed like it rained almost everyday, which made it even colder.

There was a benefit to playing in the spring. We knew we would be off in the fall, so we could go to some college and high school games if we wanted to. That's something you can't do if you're playing in the NFL. We also had the Thanksgiving and Christmas holidays off, which was really enjoyable. I really liked that aspect of playing in the USFL.

We had a real good coach in Oklahoma. Woody Widenhofer was a players' coach, no doubt about it. He never blamed a player when something went wrong. Whenever he got mad about a play, he'd tell somebody what they did wrong. But he never jumped in a player's face or anything like that. If a guy made a mistake, Woody would always pat him on the back and try to keep his spirits up. He was a great guy to play for.

We didn't have great facilities with the Outlaws. The training camp was held at some private high school. The field was real rough. The players stayed at a hotel and rode a bus to the practice field. It was like being back in high school. There was no comparison to the NFL. But it was still football.

Overall, those were some happy times for me. My peace of mind was starting to return following the death of my wife and my dealings with those assholes in Tampa. It was a chance to cool out and just be myself. Getting away like that was really good for my mental well being. And that's what I needed more than anything at that time. I really needed some emotional healing.

Going to a new city, I was pretty much by myself and had some time to think things out. I didn't really have any close friends on the team. Tampa Bay was the only team on which I made close friends. They were Jimmy Giles and Greg Roberts. Other than that, I've

My pride and joy, Ashley Monique Williams, at age two and a half.

Right. On stage with Bob Hope during his annual show saluting the college All-Americans.

Below. Youth is wonderful. In my Grambling days, I scan the field waiting for a receiver to free himself.

Below, right. On the sidelines with Robert Woods (L), one of my receivers, and James Robertson (R), a graduate assistant, during my final college game in Tokyo. After beating Temple in the final minutes, Coach Robinson called the team together in the locker room and said, "Regardless of what anybody says, the Heisman Trophy winner is here in this room."

Above. A proud day for M'Dear as she watches me receive a scroll from Louisiana Governor Edward Evans proclaiming October 15, 1977, Doug Williams Day. *Below.* At halftime of our game on Doug Williams Day. To my right is the president of Grambling, Joseph Johnson. To my left are the governor's assistant, Jim Wayne, and college football's greatest coach, Eddie Robinson.

(Photo by Allen's Studio)

My rookie year at Tampa we started to turn things around, but I took my share of lumps in the process.

Touchdowns against the Minnesota Vikings are always worth celebrating. Here joining me (from left) are Gordon Jones, Greg Roberts, and Jerry Eckwood.

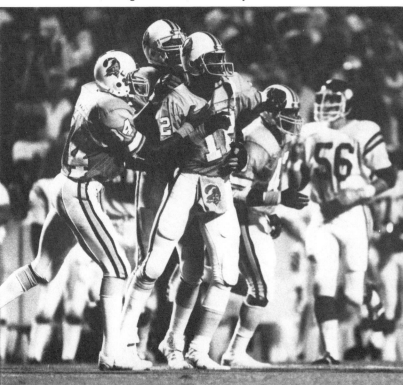

As coach of the Tampa Bay Buccaneers, John McKay usually had a lot to worry about on the sidelines. One of the many nice things about John: he didn't care if you were black, green, yellow or white, as long as you could get the job done.

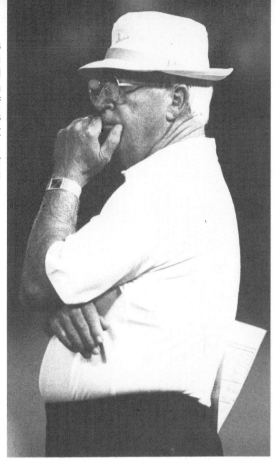

The number is the same, but the team and league are different. I was playing for the Arizona Outlaws of the now defunct USFL in 1985 when I got this pass off against the Portland Breakers.

My philosophy has always been get rid of the ball and avoid
the sack. Under pressure and moving to my right, I still manage
to get rid of the ball against the New Orleans Saints.
(Photo by John Harrelson Jr.)

Above. In the second half of the Super Bowl, Coach Gibbs had us run the ball a lot more against Denver. *Below.* A quarterback can't win a game or a Super Bowl MVP without a lot of help. Here Mark May (73) keeps the Bronco's Simon Fletcher away long enough for me to find the open man.

(Photo courtesy of Washington Redskins)

Above. The interview after the Super Bowl that stands out most in my mind is this one with Keith Jackson. As we finished Keith said, "Thank you, Sir." I think that was Keith's way of saying, "I respect you, Doug Williams."

Below. The Williams brothers at the first Doug Williams Foundation dinner. Starting from my left: My oldest brother, Robert; my youngest brother, Michael; and Manzie, whom we all call "Pop."

never been that tight with people on my own team. Things change so quickly in professional sports, you're here today and gone tomorrow. I learned that you don't get close. You just try to get along.

Playing in the USFL was pretty much like what I was used to in Tampa. We didn't have great talent on the Outlaws. I guess you could say we had some good college players. Not great college players. We had Mel Gray on one leg back then. He had played so long at St. Louis that he was barely running and couldn't stay healthy. I got my butt beat up. We didn't have a very good offensive line, so I got lots of pressure and took hits. The only difference was that the USFL didn't have the glamor of the NFL. So you got beat up and not many people noticed.

We had a rookie receiver named Al Williams, who was probably the best young talent on the team. He went on to play in the Canadian Football League and eventually played a year for the San Diego Chargers. We also had Dewey McLain, a linebacker who was part of the Atlanta Falcons' "Gritz Blitz." One of our defensive backs was Herb Williams from Baton Rouge. He played at Southern University, and now he's coaching at Capitol High School in Baton Rouge. There wasn't really much to work with on that team. Like they say, you can't make chicken salad out of chicken feathers.

A lot of the other teams in the league had better talent than we did. We had guys on our team making $23,000 or $24,000. The Outlaws were definitely one of the lowest paid teams in the league. The only players making any money were Mel Gray, Al Williams and me. Everyone else was just out there to take a shot at making it in pro football. Some of the other USFL teams went out and put together quality teams. They spent the money and ended up winning.

I think we won four or five games in Oklahoma in the 1984 season. It was similar to my first year at Tampa Bay. What made it even more difficult to take was the nasty weather in Oklahoma. It rained during eight of our nine home games. Not a drizzle, but a hard, driving rain. And when we played in Chicago, there was a blizzard. You never knew what to expect.

The highlight of the season was beating the Michigan Panthers and the Houston Gamblers. The Panthers had Anthony Carter, Bobby Hebert and some other really good players. We played them in Tulsa, and it was pouring down rain and freezing cold that day. We just kept coming at them and took advantage of some turnovers, and we finally beat them.

It was raining again when we played Houston. The Gamblers had Jim Kelly and their run-and-shoot offense. We were behind by fifteen points with about three minutes to go, and we came back to win on a Hail Mary pass that I threw to Al Williams. Those were big upsets, but we didn't have many more like that.

Tulsa just wasn't large enough to have a professional football team. It's a very nice city, but too small for what the USFL needed. The fan support just wasn't there. At least in Tampa, we had large crowds and great interest in the team, even when we weren't winning.

After the 1984 season, the Outlaws and the Arizona Wranglers merged and became the Arizona Outlaws. That meant I would again have to relocate, and I didn't really want to move to Arizona. At the time, I felt I had moved enough. Within a year's time, I had moved from Tampa back to Zachary and from Zachary to Tulsa. And now a few months later, I was going to have to pack up and head way out west to Phoenix.

It was always hot in Arizona. We couldn't even practice during the day, because the sun and heat would kill you. So we had meetings during the day and started practice around five or six in the afternoon. It was still about 100 degrees when we went out on the field, but at least the sun wasn't right over your head.

I told Bill Tatham that I didn't like it and didn't want to stay. Then he started saying how great the weather was. He said it hardly ever rains, there's no humidity, and the sun shines every day. I told him, "That's great for some people, Bill, but I don't really need to work on my tan."

Besides that, Arizona is Barry Goldwater country. I wasn't too excited about living in his state. And Evan Meacham was going to run for governor. So that wasn't a good situation for a black quarterback from the South. Everyone knew what kind of person Meacham is. Anyone who doesn't want to recognize a holiday for Martin Luther King is obviously a bigot. Meacham was very open about the fact he's a racist. And most of the people out there must have felt the same way or else he wouldn't have been elected. Not only was he a bigot, but he was corrupt, too. That's why they finally had to get rid of him. He was just Goldwater's boy anyway.

No black wants to live in Barry Goldwater's state. Arizona belongs to Goldwater. The biggest department store in that area is Goldwater's. I remember walking through the Fiesta Mall in Tempe one afternoon and I saw only two black people in the whole place. And it was a pretty big mall. In Phoenix, the black population may be 5 percent. You get to Tempe, and it's a lot lower than that. Once you get to Scottsdale, it's right at 0 percent.

It's really better for blacks in the South. At least you know who you're dealing with in the South. You know who are the bigots. In Arizona, it's not as obvious. They're more secretive about it. Personally, I'd rather have somebody tell me that he doesn't like me because I'm black, instead of sneaking behind my back and hating me.

I decided to rent a house with Ernest Anderson, the running back from Oklahoma State. We got along well, so at least I had somebody to talk to out there. When Ernest wasn't around, I had to try hard to find somebody to spend time with. I went to the movies, went out to eat a lot and tried to find whatever entertainment I could find. I ate a lot of ice cream that spring. I fell in love with rum raisin. At least five days a week, I'd go to this ice cream store and buy some rum raisin.

Phoenix didn't support the Outlaws very well. One reason was that Phoenix wanted to get an NFL franchise, and I think they thought it would hurt their chances of getting an NFL team if the USFL was successful. There was a negative attitude about our team. I know they didn't want us around. Our training facility wasn't the greatest. It was an abandoned high school that had been renovated. It did have some tennis courts and basketball courts, and we had plenty of room. But it was still a high school. The funny thing is the Phoenix Cardinals are using that same facility today.

The best thing about the merger was we picked up some better players. We had some veterans like Carl Lorch, Bruce Laird and a few others. We had a decent team, but didn't do much better because some of the other teams merged and improved their talent.

Arizona was fortunate to have a good head coach in Frank Kush. I had heard all the stories about his troubles at Arizona State, but I got along great with him. Frank and I never had any problems.

Let me tell you, Kush is one heck of a disciplinarian. He doesn't believe in making mistakes. I remember one time we were getting ready for a game, Al Williams (still our best receiver), had a couple of busted assignments. Kush turned to one of his assistants and said, "Get his ass out of there. He's not going to play this week."

I couldn't believe he would pull our best receiver out of the lineup. I thought, "Oh my gosh, if Al doesn't play, we're really going to be in trouble. I won't have anyone to throw it to." Kush finally relented and let Al play in the game. But he got his message across.

Kush was straight with his players. He told you what he wanted and that was the only way he would accept it. Even though he was demanding, he was fair.

I'll never forget what he made us do on Mondays. You're talking about the day after the game, and he made all the players run two miles. But the most intriguing thing about it was that Frank Kush led the run. We had to follow him around. It was amazing. He kept himself in good shape, and he made sure all of his players were in good shape.

Kush turned us into a decent team. But we still weren't good enough to win our division or get into the playoffs. We moved up a little bit, but we were still in the middle of the pack.

Our best game of the season was against the New Jersey Generals and Herschel Walker. We played them on national TV, and it was a big game for us. On that day, we just couldn't do anything wrong. Ron Willow took a screen pass, which was almost intercepted, and ran sixty yards for a touchdown. Our defense really played well. We held Herschel to less than fifty yards, and we upset the Generals.

We also had a chance to beat the Houston Gamblers for the second straight year. Everything went right for us in the first half, and we had a big lead. But to start the second half, we kicked off to Clarence Verdin, and he ran it back ninety-some yards for a touchdown. We never should have kicked off to Clarence. Everything went downhill after that, and we ended up losing. They got their run-and-shoot going, and we were gone.

Every game was hot in Phoenix, but the one that really stands out was when we played Portland. It was one of those afternoons when the sun was blazing and the temperature was over 100 degrees. I had trouble seeing my receivers, because the glare was right in my eyes all the time.

We had one interesting off-field incident during that season. They had booked us on a commercial flight, instead of a charter. So that meant we had about fifty professional football players mixed in with the general public. What happened was one of our players, Donnie Hickman, got in an argument with one of the defensive coaches, Bill Terlick, who coaches for Cleveland now. We had lost the game, and Coach Terlick blamed the offense for causing the loss. Hickman, who was an offensive lineman, disagreed with what the coach had said, and they got in a heated argument over it. Then they started fighting right in the middle of a bunch of passengers. Hickman whipped the coach real bad. Someone finally broke it up, but it was a bad situation. I know the airline got a lot of complaints about it. We shouldn't have been flying commercial. Basketball and baseball teams can get away with it, because you're dealing with smaller numbers. But when you've got a full football squad, you can't mix them in with the public like that. The NFL would never do that.

The frustrating thing about the USFL was being overlooked. The media didn't pay any attention to the league. We didn't get the kind of coverage that the NFL gets. That killed the league.

At that point, I was ready to get out of the USFL. The league was in financial trouble anyway. It seemed doomed to fail, especially when they decided to move the season to the fall. I thought it was going to be awfully hard, if not impossible, to go head to head with the NFL. After all, we got such poor coverage playing in the spring, and it was bound to go down in the fall because everything would be focused on the NFL.

I think most of the USFL's owners were just trying to hang in there as long as they could. It was evident they were losing money. I think they were banking on the lawsuit against the NFL. I'm sure they were hoping to recover enough money to keep the USFL afloat.

Donald Trump and some of the other wealthy USFL owners were also a big part of the downfall of the league. Trump bought Herschel Walker, Doug Flutie and players like that. Those kind of owners were outbidding some of the others who couldn't afford to pay high prices for a lot of the best athletes. A few of the teams, like Michigan, Oakland and New Jersey, were stockpiling all the talent. They put out millions of dollars and got the best players. Whereas, Bill Tatham and guys like him had some money, but not enough to just throw it around. I don't blame them for not blowing their money. The L.A. Express gave Steve Young $40 million. That's ridiculous. Those kind of owners were a major cause of the death of the USFL.

The NFL had something to do with it, too. There's no doubt in my mind that the NFL conspired to shut down the USFL. The NFL is capable of doing a lot of things. I don't know anything that it can't do. That's one organization that has tremendous power, probably more than any other professional sports league in the world. The owners and general managers in the NFL work closely together on everything. If they want something done, it's only a phone call away from getting done. They've got all the power in their hands, believe me.

It was a joke the way the lawsuit between the two leagues came out. The USFL didn't get anything from the NFL. I think it was totally unfair to award a dollar to the USFL. All they were doing was poking fun at the league. It would have been better to find the NFL guilty and not award anything at all than to give them a dollar. The NFL wouldn't let the USFL operate, so it should have paid a price for doing that. Now the NFL is starting the International Football League. That's the same thing as the USFL, except it's overseas.

With all that going on, I was ready to move on. Everything was a struggle. But it was still a source of employment for a lot of football players and coaches. That's what I hated about the league closing down. So many people lost their jobs. It's a shame, because some of them deserved to be playing professional football. Maybe they just didn't get a break in the NFL. But they could still play football.

The financial problems of the league didn't affect me. The Tathams paid me everything I was owed. I never missed a paycheck in my two seasons in the USFL. Then as part of a settlement after the league folded, they agreed to build my house in Zachary. According to my contract, they had to pay me $500,000 over a ten-year period. I didn't really want $50,000 a year, because I figured what's $50,000 going to be worth ten years from now. I wanted to get the money right then. So what we did was settle for half of what they owed me, which is about what it cost to build my house.

After that, I knew my football career might be over. But I had played seven years, made some money, and was ready to get on with my life. My goal has always been to become a coach, and that's what I set out to do. I had a beautiful new home, and I was glad to be back in Zachary so I could spend more time with Ashley and the rest of my family.

In 1985, I was still under contract with the USFL, which planned to play football that fall. That meant I had to sit around and wait. What I did was become a volunteer coach at Southern University. They had me work with the wide receivers. It was a good opportunity to learn about the coaching profession. I started to check into permanent coaching positions.

I'm a realist. I try to deal with life the way it is. At that time, the facts were I wasn't in pro football anymore and nobody was knocking down my door trying to get me. So I didn't worry about it. I could have gone to coach at Bishop College, and I'm sure they would have given me a job at Grambling. But I decided to coach at Southern, so I could live at home.

That year at Southern was a great experience. It was a tremendous learning time. I began to develop ideas about the kind of people with whom I would want to work, what kind of coaching I would like to do, how to deal with problems concerning athletic department management, what kind of athletes to recruit and how to deal with them. It was amazing. It certainly wasn't what I expected.

In college coaching, you have to be so many different things. Sometimes you have to be a counselor, sometimes a momma, sometimes a daddy, and sometimes you have to be an ass kicker. When I say an ass kicker, I mean you have to get on the guy's case. Not physically, but mentally. You have to let him know he's not doing right and this is what you have to do if you want to be something in life. I really learned a lot about the coaching profession.

But part of me wanted to get back into the NFL. I missed the competition, and there was good money to be made. One drawback was the Bucs still held the rights to me. Even though I was considered a free agent, any team that signed me would have to compensate the Bucs with a player or draft choice. That's a ridiculous rule. I hadn't played in the NFL in over three years, and if I came back to the league, some team still owned me. That's not football, that's slavery.

After what happened in my previous negotiations with the Bucs, I decided against using an agent to represent me. I knew the NFL general managers could get in touch with me if they wanted me. But no team even gave me a call during the 1985 season and into the 1986 exhibition season. I was starting to wonder if the NFL was going to forget about Doug Williams. I'm sure the Bucs loved it. They wanted to see me left out to rot.

• *12*

Return to the NFL

When the USFL folded in 1986, a lot of the USFL's quarterbacks were picked up. The New Orleans Saints won a bidding war for Bobby Hebert. Jim Kelly went to Buffalo. The Tampa Bay Buccaneers got Steve Young. None of those guys had ever played in the NFL.

Even Chuck Fusina, my former backup at Tampa Bay, was picked up by the Green Bay Packers. Chuck was a guy who didn't have great ability, but he was a real smart player. Playing for Jim Mora in the USFL, Chuck was in the right system to utilize his capabilties. They did a lot of checking off and then threw short passes. You can hide somebody's flaws in a system like that. That's the only way Chuck could have made it.

Twenty-eight NFL teams went to training camp in 1986. Not one offered to give me a tryout, much less a contract. Was Doug Williams blackballed by the NFL? I can't say that for certain because I don't know what went on in the front offices of all those teams. It seems logical that at least one team would have expressed interest in me unless they had a legitimate reason not to do so.

I'm sure some of them would say they had reasons. But I was a healthy thirty-one-year-old quarterback with plenty of good years ahead of me. There was no logical reason to leave me alone. I had proven myself in the NFL, and I belonged back in the league. A lot of teams like to keep experienced quarterbacks around as backups because they're capable of coming off the bench and performing.

I would have been even more valuable to the Saints. I grew up in Louisiana. I played high school and college football in Louisiana. My family and friends lived in Louisiana. The Saints wanted Hebert for the same reasons. I would have been the perfect backup. The ironic thing is the Saints talked to Fusina about being their backup, and they ended up signing Babe Laufenberg as their third quarterback. Well, Laufenberg was the quarterback who the Redskins cut after they eventually brought me to camp. That shows how the Saints operate.

I've never even received a phone call from Jim Mora, Jim Finks or any past front office personnel of the Saints. Not one. The Saints could have drafted me in 1978. They could have signed me after my contract with the Bucs ran out in 1982. And they could have signed me after the USFL folded. But they never bothered to talk to me. The bottom line is the New Orleans Saints aren't ready for a black quarterback. Jim Finks is one of the NFL's good ol' boys. He may never sign a black quarterback.

The Saints, and a lot of other NFL teams, were interested in Fusina. They welcomed him back to the league with open arms. After all, he was a quarterback who had experience in two leagues. But so was I. Why would any team pick Chuck ahead of me? He's white, and I'm not. In my mind, that's the only possible reason he was signed and I wasn't. I mean he was my backup. Why do you think Chuck sat on the bench while I played at Tampa Bay?

I do know for certain that the Tampa Bay Bucs did not want Doug Williams back in the NFL. I've got proof of that. A team official with the Washington Redskins told me that Phil Krueger, the Bucs general manager, called Joe Gibbs and tried to convince him not to sign me. In fact, he called Coach Gibbs a couple of times. That's called blackballing a player, pure and simple.

I wouldn't be surprised if Krueger called other coaches and general managers to persuade them not to contact me. That's just the type of person that Phil Krueger is. And I'm sure Hugh Culverhouse would have done the same thing. He probably told Krueger to do it.

On August 12, I finally got the call to come back to the NFL, despite everything the Bucs had tried to do to stop it. Coach Gibbs called me at home in Zachary. Like always, he was very business-like and got right to the point.

"Douglas," he said. "We would like to have you with the Redskins. I don't know about the money. I'm sure you can work that out with our general manager, Bobby Beathard. All I need to know is can you play backup quarterback? We've already committed to Jay Schroeder as our starter. So would you be interested in being our backup quarterback?"

"Sure, Coach," I answered without hesitating a moment. "I don't have a job right now. I can play anywhere you want me to play."

That was about all Coach Gibbs had to say. He hung up, and a few minutes later, Beathard called me about a contract. They had already been in training camp for a couple weeks, so they wanted to get me signed up in a hurry. I wasn't that concerned about the money. I mainly just wanted to play and get a chance to show that I could still get the job done in the NFL.

I didn't want to use an agent any more, because I thought I could best represent myself. After the Bucs' fiasco, I wanted to know everything that was going on during the negotiation. Dealing with the Redskins was entirely different than the Bucs. Beathard told me that they wanted to give me a three-year contract with a salary of $375,000 for the first year, $400,000 for the second and $425,000 for the third. I didn't want to take their first offer, so I asked for $425,000, $450,000 and $475,000. Beathard said he'd have to get back to me. The next day, he called and said the Redskins would meet my request. So we had a deal just like that.

When I reported to camp, the Redskins had Schroeder, Mark Rypien and Laufenberg as their quarterbacks. The competition wasn't anything I couldn't handle, but the Redskins' system wasn't the easiest in the world. It was almost like starting over again as a professional. They had completely different terminology and highly complex offensive schemes. Coach Gibbs spends a lot of hours on that blackboard, so there's a great deal for the quarterbacks to learn. He prepares his team as well as anybody in football. If anyone prepares his team better than Joe Gibbs, he's doing a lot of work and a heck of a job.

It was so refreshing to join the Washington Redskins. It was like night and day compared to what I had been used to. The Redskins are a classy organization. Going to that team after what I had been a part of in Tampa was an amazing experience. Tampa is not even close to the Redskins. Not anywhere close. It's hard to believe they play in the same league. From the trainers to the equipment managers to the office people, the Redskins are a professional, top-rate organization. Everybody feels that he or she is a part of that operation. They make sure you feel that way. They do everything they can to make you feel important. That's such a good feeling.

I can't believe there's a more classy organization in any sport. You call everyone by their first names. And they all speak to you and ask you how you've been doing. They're interested in your well being. They're concerned about you as a person, not just a performer or a commodity. It's a family atmosphere.

In Tampa, they had signs up that read, "Employees Only," so you couldn't walk down certain halls. You couldn't stop by the office and say hello to the secretaries or office staff. You had to have a specific reason or an appointment to come by. And at lunch time, you had forty-five minutes or an hour, and you had to get in your car and drive somewhere to get something to eat.

In Washington, you come out of a team meeting and your lunch is waiting for you on the table. You don't have to leave the complex to get something to eat. It's provided for you. After Thursday practices, you've got someone there with all kinds of goodies to eat. On Friday, you've either got pizza or sub sandwiches. And on Saturday morning, you walk in for the meetings, and you've got doughnuts and milk waiting there for you. It's just like being at home.

When I first arrived in town, they helped me get settled and tried to make me feel at home in the area. They introduced me to everyone in the organization. They helped me make moving arrangements. They helped me find a car, and then they told me where to look for apartments and helped me set that up. They took care of everything I needed to live there.

They want to make you feel as comfortable as possible. All they want you to do is work for them. They take care of everything else. That's the way to run a successful business, and it's obviously a good way to run a football team. I think that's a big part of why the Redskins are winners. It's a team effort all the way down the line.

The Redskins are owned by Jack Kent Cooke, and his son John

handles the day-to-day operations. Jack is very arrogant, aggressive, authoritative and just a great businessman. Jack wants it his way, and he usually gets it. He's the E.F. Hutton type of guy: When he speaks, he wants you to listen. Still, you can't compare Jack Kent Cooke with Hugh Culverhouse. It's a completely different class of people.

Jack tries hard to make sure the people working for him are happy. I think he does a good job of that. The Redskins have never had a problem paying the players who produce for them. They don't try to cheat you out of anything. If you produce, they'll take care of you. That's just good business, and Jack is a great businessman.

I think John is dictated to by his father. John tries hard to run the business like he thinks it should be run and like he thinks his father wants it run. He's got a lot of his dad's traits. Both of the Cookes are fair men. They're good people to be associated with.

Throughout their ranks, the Redskins have the best organization you can imagine. You can feel free to talk to anyone in the organization from the secretaries up to Jack and John. All you have to do is knock on John's door, and he's ready to talk to you. And Bobby Mitchell, the assistant general manager, is right next door to John. Then you've got Charlie Casserly right down the hall, and his door is always open. I didn't take up much of their time, because I'm the type of player that doesn't believe in getting too close to management. They've got a job to do, and I've got a job to do. I always feel it's best to keep a distance. I don't think players should socialize with management. That doesn't mean you can't be friendly and get along with one another.

I'm closer to Bobby Mitchell than any other management person. Bobby is different. Since he was a player himself, he knows more about what the players' needs are. He's a great businessman himself, but he also understands how to deal with the players on a personal basis. Away from the office, he's a friend of mine. We work together a lot in the community. Bobby was one of the greatest receivers and running backs to ever play the game, so he's very well known in the community. If somebody wants me to do something, they usually call Bobby. We do a lot of it together.

The Redskins fans are really special, too. It's a tradition in Washington. These people know the game of football. When you've got a stadium that holds only 55,000 and the waiting list for season tickets is 30,000 or 35,000 long, it lets you know what kind of interest the team generates. The Redskins have a top caliber franchise in every regard.

When I first saw Jay Schroeder, I was shocked to see how big he was. I had never seen him before, and let me tell you, Jay is a big man. He's about 6-5, 210 pounds and has a strong arm. At that point, I could understand why Coach Gibbs wanted him to be his starting quarterback. I totally accepted my role as his backup. Jay had played well after Joe Theismann got hurt. And he was young and had a bright future ahead of him. He was the obvious choice for the starter, at least until I learned the system.

Jay and I didn't ever get very close, so I don't know that much about him. But I could sense right from the beginning that he felt threatened by me. I was somebody who had been successful in the league and could do some things pretty well. You could see Jay was a little unnerved by my presence. But he played fairly well in 1986. He led us to the playoffs and made the Pro Bowl. Of course, he was surrounded by tremendous talent. People like Art Monk, Gary Clark and the Hogs made Jay Schroeder look good.

In some ways, it was difficult being a backup, especially since I had never been in that position as a pro. Naturally, I wanted to play. What made it difficult to accept was the fact I knew I could do as well or better than Schroeder. It got to me a little bit, but I was able to roll with the punches. It was somewhat easier because I had been told from the start that I would be the backup. That was my position. That was where they wanted me to play, and it was up to me to make the most of it.

The thing that kept me going was playing for the scout team in practice and competing against our No. 1 defense every day. That meant I was throwing against people like Darrell Green. I was fortunate to have receivers like Ricky Sanders and Clarence Verdin. Those were the best receivers I had played with since college. Both of these guys are starters in the NFL now. Ricky is still with the Redskins, and Clarence is with the Indianapolis Colts.

That was a heck of a scout team we had. Some days, we killed our first defense. We had a great time playing against them. I played my games every day of the week. That really helped keep my interest up. I loved playing against our defense, and they got a lot out of it, too. We really got them pumped up to play.

I guess it was a good thing that I had practices to look forward to, because Coach Gibbs doesn't believe in playing two quarterbacks. The only game I got into was against Dallas. It was so far out of reach that it didn't matter. We were ahead 41-14 when they put me in late in the game. I threw one pass, and it was incomplete. So my final stats for the season were 0 for 1 and 0 yards.

Since I wasn't getting to play, I became a cheerleader on the side-lines. I wanted to do whatever I could to help the team and get involved in the game. Coach Gibbs just believes in going with one quarterback if he's doing the job. I had to accept that if I was going to be content with the Redskins.

But being a competitor, I couldn't really be satisfied sitting on the bench. I wanted to be out there leading the team like I always had in the past. For a while, I thought about asking to be traded.

Even though I wasn't happy with my playing time, it was great to be back in the NFL again, and it was even better to be on a winning team. Any time you're winning, it's a great feeling. I really got involved in the team, even though I wasn't playing. I tried to give our defense a real live look every day in practice. I took my assignment to heart. I tried to play every practice like a game. I didn't throw bad passes. It was a game-type situation to me, and I was the leader of our scout team. By taking that approach, I think I gained the respect of my teammates. I was a veteran who had been a starter for a long time, but I was taking practice seriously. I wanted to do everything I could to make the Redskins successful.

We got into the playoffs as a wild-card team and beat the Los Angeles Rams in the wild-card game. That put us up against the Bears, who had just won the Super Bowl, and we had to play in Chicago. But Jim McMahon was hurt, and they had to play Doug Flutie. He threw two or three interceptions, because he wasn't tall enough to see over the linemen. We ended up winning that game, and it put us in the NFC championship game. Our opponent was a familiar one. We had to play the New York Giants, who won our division. And the championship game was in Giants Stadium.

At that point, it didn't matter to me that I wasn't playing. When it came to the championship game, you just wanted to be there. The name of the game is getting to the Super Bowl. There are a lot of guys who have been to the Super Bowl and never played a down. Cliff

Stoudt has three Super Bowl rings and never played. You can never take away those rings. I just wanted to make it to the Super Bowl myself.

The Giants were a great football team that year. They had Lawrence Taylor, Joe Morris and Phil Simms, among many others. And they were operating on all cylinders. They were playing like Super Bowl champions, and that's what they eventually became. The Giants beat us 17-0 and went on to beat Denver, 39-20, in the Super Bowl. It was the second time I had made it to the NFC championship game and missed out on a chance to go to the Super Bowl.

That season, I learned right away that one of the most important reasons for the Redskins' success is Joe Gibbs. Coach Gibbs is a players' coach. A lot of the time he'd take the blame when we lost games, even though it wasn't his fault. He just isn't the type to point fingers at the players. What he'd do is tell us to take a long, hard look at the game film. Then he would say, ''You figure out if you could have done more to help us win.'' He'd get us to evaluate ourselves and reach down for more.

Another thing about Coach Gibbs is his thoroughness. He covers every little detail of the game. He makes sure nothing is overlooked. In meetings, he goes over every situation. The quarterbacks get the most information. We'd study that game plan until there were no questions. We would go over first down plays, second and long, second and short, third and long, and third and short. In every situation, he lets you know what could possibly happen. Who has a certain blitz pickup. What we're supposed to do if the linebackers come. All those things have to be carefully reviewed. We'd cover everything with a fine tooth comb, and Coach Gibbs made sure you were just as aware of it as he was.

You have to be mentally alert at all times to play for the Redskins. In practice, you have to devote total concentration to what's going on, just like you would in a game. Your mind has to be completely on what's happening on the field or you'll get lost. If you're standing back behind the huddle talking to someone, you can get lost in a hurry.

Practices are really complicated. It's serious business. We would prepare for exactly what we thought the other team's defense was going to do. We'd work on who would pick up blitzes by the safety or the two outside linebackers. And everyone got a chance to react to the different situations they might face in a game. That way we were all prepared to play.

Joe Gibbs works hard to try to be the best at what he does. I don't think he could possibly do any more to help the team. He comes in to Redskins Park on Monday and doesn't leave until Thursday night. All day long and most of the night, he's working on finding a way to win the game. Then he'll get some sleep in his office and start all over again in the morning. I'm not going to say Joe Gibbs is the best coach in the game, but he's the best that I know of.

Going to Washington was the best move I ever made. I love that city. The only thing I hated about playing in Washington was that I didn't start my career there. I wish I had played my whole career there. If there's a city made for Doug Williams, it has to be Washington, D.C. I think that's where I belonged all along.

First of all, the city's population is 75 percent black. So I had an awful lot of fans right from the start. Plus, I got a chance to meet so many people. I guess I immediately became a role model for the kids. I liked being in that position. It made me feel good that I was appreciated and thought well of. And I wanted to be a role model. I wanted to set an example for the kids and show them how to be a leader, not a follower.

There's so much to see and do in Washington, too. You can do whatever you think you want to do in that city. It's got so much to offer. I lived in the Virginia suburbs, but I often went into the city for various functions. If you want to ride in a limo to a different function every night, you can do that. If you want to go to a nice restaurant every night, you can do that. If you want to go on a sightseeing tour, you could do that. It's a great place to learn about American history. Those are the types of things that D.C. has to offer.

Mainly, I liked to go into town for a good meal at one of the nicer restaurants. My favorites are seafood at Chrisfield, ribs at Houston's and Cajun food at Copeland's. At other times, I'd go to Blues Alley in Georgetown to listen to musicians like Phyllis Hyman and Noel Pointer. Occasionally, I'd go out to a nightclub or something like that.

During my first year in D.C., I was asked to take part in the Redskins "12th Man" video. The Chicago Bears had been very successful with their video, so I guess someone decided the Redskins needed to make one. Most of the players had a part in it. There were also scenes with the fans and highlights from the games. I had a couple of speaking parts. It was all in rap. Karen Kauffman, the wife of one of the players, arranged it, along with a young lady named Lisa Robinson.

Lisa reminded me of my first wife. She had that sweet, warm personality that made you feel good to be around her. She was a young and attractive woman. Mainly what I liked about her was the way she acted. But at the time, I didn't know it was just an act. Lisa was a great saleswoman. That was her business. She worked for Xerox, and she knew what it took to sell you something. This was a city girl. She's from Detroit and went to school at Howard University in Washington. So she was a sharp girl, no doubt about it.

Let me tell you, she was good at selling herself. She portrayed exactly the kind of woman that she knew I was looking for. A great wife and companion for me. A loving mother for Ashley. She knew how much I loved my daughter, and she understood that would be a major factor in who I decided to date or get serious about. So she became just that type of woman, and she sold me on it.

We started going out a lot on dates. We enjoyed the same kind of things, such as plays and movies. And we went out to eat quite a bit. We just spent a lot of time together. She seemed like just what I was looking for, and we were very happy together.

Then early in 1987, she called me one night crying and saying she was pregnant. She kept telling me that she didn't want to be pregnant without being married. I wasn't ready to get married. I hadn't even thought about marrying Lisa up to that point. So I told her that I didn't want to do it.

But she insisted that she wasn't going to have the baby unless I married her. It was all new to me. I had never been in the position of having a girlfriend get pregnant. After she continued to cry and cry, I couldn't help but feel sorry for her. So I told her, ''All right, Lisa, we'll do something about it. We'll get married.''

The more I thought about it, the more I knew it was the appropriate thing to do. Lisa was pregnant with my baby, and I should go ahead and marry her. That was the right thing to do, and I knew it.

About a month later, Lisa told me that she had had a miscarriage and lost the baby. It was still early enough that I could have backed out on marrying her. But I felt that I had made a commitment to her, and I believe in living up to my commitments.

Now that I look back on the situation, it's easy to see that I played the sucker. But I'm human. I just let her get to me emotionally. I never thought I would let that happen to me, but I did. It just goes to show you that you can't feel sorry for some people.

Part of our agreement was that we would live in my house in Zachary. I didn't want to live there for half the year and then have to close up the house for the other half of the year while I had to be in Washington to play football. Plus, I didn't want to move Ashley all around. So we agreed that Lisa would stay in Zachary during the season and come see me in Washington on the weekends or come stay for a week at a time whenever she wanted. But she was going to spend most of her time in Zachary taking care of Ashley. And that was fine with her. She was totally agreeable to that idea.

We got married in June and spent the summer in Zachary. I could tell right away that Lisa didn't want to be there. She made it clear that she'd rather move back to D.C. But I told her that we had agreed on living in Louisiana. That's where I enjoy being. My idea is that I work in D.C.—that's just where my job is. My home is Zachary, and I didn't want to be moving everything every six months or so. That wasn't feasible to me.

The real reason Lisa wanted to be in Washington was to be in the limelight. She didn't want to miss any of the social events. Even when she was living in Zachary, she was on the phone most of the time talking to her friends back in D.C. All that they talked about was gossip, and that's something I never liked. I didn't like it in Tampa when a lot of the players' wives wanted to be talking about what everyone else was doing. They just gossip about things that aren't any of their business, like other players and their wives. I don't think that's right, and I didn't want Lisa to be a part of that.

Even that didn't bother me as much as her attitude. Lisa changed so much after we got married. I found out what she was really like, and it was so different than the sweet little thing that she wanted me to think she was. I discovered that she has one of the worst attitudes of anyone I've ever been associated with. She just can't get along with other people. I don't care who it is.

Lisa argued with everyone, especially on the telephone. She felt like everything had to be her way. She was so headstrong. Sometimes that's good if you use it the right way. But she was just impossible to deal with.

The strange thing was the way she looked at our marriage. I had agreed to marry her because I thought she was pregnant, and I had some money and was taking good care of her. When we first met, Lisa was in deep financial trouble. She didn't have a pot to piss in or a window to throw it out of. She was living in an apartment and was about $2,500 in debt with credit cards. I took care of all that for her. I paid everything off. A lot of her friends told her that she should feel lucky to be married to Doug Williams.

But that wasn't the way she looked at it at all. She had the attitude that I should feel lucky to be married to her. Lisa thought she was better than everyone else.

Lisa was just a very negative person. She spent most of her time trying to find out bad things about people—anything that they had done wrong. She never took a positive approach, and that's why she was always unhappy.

The real problem for Lisa was her upbringing. Her parents split up when she was twelve years old, and that really affected her. She's always had problems with her parents. Because her mother didn't get along with her father, Lisa wouldn't have anything to do with her father. She didn't get back in touch with her dad until she was getting ready to get married.

Her father lives in Ruston, Louisiana, and Lisa decided he should give her away at the wedding. But when her mother found out, she said she wasn't going to come to the wedding. I told Lisa, "That's fine. If she doesn't want to come, send her pictures. We don't need her there if she's going to act like that." After all, they weren't paying for the wedding. I was paying for everything, so I didn't think her parents had a right to mess things up. Her mother finally agreed to come.

With all the problems over the wedding, our marriage was on bad terms from the start. And it just got worse and worse. I think the biggest problem was money.

We had been married only two days when Lisa started complaining about money. She told me she had this CPA friend who said we should pool our money. Lisa was working at Xerox at the time. Her friend suggested that we should each put in 10 percent of our salary to pay the bills. At that time, I was making $450,000 with the Redskins, and she was probably making something like $25,000. I told her, "You've got to be kidding. Ten percent of my salary is $45,000, and 10 percent of yours is only a couple thousand. That's not fair. Tell your friend to mind her own business. She's not going to run our household."

Lisa always wanted to get her hands on my money. Always. The main thing she wanted was to get her hands on my checkbook. It really bothered her that I took care of that. And when there was a business matter that I didn't have time to handle, my mother did it for me. Lisa used to always make little comments about my mom handling my money. It really troubled her.

Going into the marriage, I knew there could be a problem, so we had a prenuptial agreement drawn up. Basically, it stated that whatever I had before the marriage was mine and whatever she had before the marriage was hers, and whatever we accumulated together would be ours. Another part of it stated that she wouldn't get anything from my contract with the Redskins or any future contracts. That was settled before we got married. She never saw one of my payroll checks from the Redskins.

I think every professional athlete has to do something like that. You've got to protect yourself, because nowadays you can't take a chance. You never know what a woman is really thinking about. That may sound bad to the women, but that's tough. It's the truth. And women should feel the same way if they have some money. You just have to be aware that there are some people who are just out to get money. You have to be aware of what a woman is looking for. She's going to want you to believe it's just love. I love you, I love you, I love you. But "I love you" doesn't pay the bills. Quite naturally, if a woman sees a good situation, she's going to love you to death, and she's going to tell you whatever she thinks you want to hear.

The bottom line is Lisa was one of those women who wanted dollars. And it killed her that she didn't have a free reign over my check book. That was what drove us apart. If I had given her all the money she wanted, she would have been as happy as can be. But I don't believe in throwing it away.

Our problems with money started right with the wedding. She wanted all these extra things. Candlelight dinners and all kinds of expensive things. She was running up the bill. But I said, "Wait a minute, Lisa. You can scratch all that stuff out. We're not going to do any of it." That money was coming out of my pocket, and I wasn't going to let her throw it away.

Lisa was such a schemer. She was running up thousands of dollars in credit-card debt, just like she did before we got married. So she gave me her credit cards and I paid them off again. I thought that was the end of it. But she found a way to keep charging things.

One day, I was at home looking up a number in the phone book, and in the very back, I found all these account numbers written down. What Lisa had done was call the stores that she had accounts with and got them to tell her the account numbers. So she was ordering everything by phone. When she came home that day, I took her credit cards and gave them back to her. I told her, "You might as well keep these. It doesn't do any good to take them away, because I see that you're just charging everything by phone."

She didn't say anything. What could she say? Everything I told her was the truth.

Lisa was a big-time operator. If there was a way to get something out of someone, she would figure out how to do it. She's just real sharp. She's strictly a business person. Money is the most important thing to her.

During her second pregnancy, she really got me angry when she went on a shopping spree for maternity clothes. She ordered some outfits from a private boutique in Washington, and I found out her three dresses cost $2,200. I told her, "Hold on a minute. I didn't marry no woman to sit home while you're pregnant and wear clothes that cost $2,200." We feuded for days over that. I got so mad I didn't speak to her for two weeks. She finally sent them back.

Everything continued to build up during that summer. After I went to training camp in July, Lisa kept telling me she wanted to come live in Washington permanently. There weren't enough parties and social gatherings to attend in Zachary to suit her. She couldn't drive the Mercedes to the nightclubs in Georgetown and wear fancy evening gowns to the Kennedy Center. Zachary wasn't high brow enough to suit her. And she didn't try to learn to like it. Zachary is a great place to live. But not for Lisa.

After five months, Lisa decided she was going to leave. So she packed up and went home to Detroit to live with her mother. We talked on the phone some during the 1987 season, but there really wasn't much point to it. Lisa wasn't going to be content unless she had a lot of money and a lot of opportunities to flaunt it. I knew then that it had been a mistake to marry her. She wasn't anything like the woman I thought I had married. She certainly wasn't anything like my first wife. I felt I had been let down and deceived.

13

Super Season

I wasn't too excited about the prospects of backing up Jay Schroeder again in 1987. I was glad to be back in the NFL, but I wanted to play. It was particularly hard to take when I had a much better preseason than Schroeder and still remained the No. 2 quarterback. There just didn't seem to be any hope of playing for the Redskins.

Don't get me wrong, I still loved being in Washington, and I didn't think there was a better organization in the league than the Redskins. I also knew the Redskins were going to have a great team and had a good chance of going to the Super Bowl. We had some great talent on that football team and some of it hadn't even been tapped yet. They hadn't played Ricky Sanders yet. There were just so many good football players on the team. We had Kelvin Bryant, who was probably the best third-down back in the game. We had Art Monk and Gary Clark as receivers. George Rogers was still running the ball pretty well, and we had the Hogs up front. They were a great offensive line. On defense, Dexter Manley and Charles Mann were probably the two best pass rushers in the league, and Dave Butz and Darryl Grant gave us strength in the middle. Then you had Darrell Green and Barry Wilburn in the secondary. We believed we were going to get back in the playoffs, and then it would be our year. The Redskins are a different team in the playoffs. We felt if we could get there, we could always turn it up a notch. It was great to be on a team like that.

But as a competitive athlete, I didn't want to sit around for another year and watch somebody else play. Cheerleading was fun for a while, but I wanted to be a starter again. I really had to get out there and play.

Even before we went to training camp, I talked to Coach Gibbs about how much I wanted to play, and he understood completely. He told me if something came along that was beneficial to Doug Williams and beneficial to the Redskins, he would work something out. He understood that I didn't want to go anywhere they were trying to build a team. I didn't want to leave just to be leaving.

All indications were I would be traded during the 1987 season. It had been in the wind for a while that the Los Angeles Raiders wanted to make a deal for me. Nobody had talked directly to me, but I found out about it. A lot of people thought it was going to happen.

After we played the Rams in a preseason game out in L.A., Coach Gibbs called me at home Monday morning to let me know there was a possibility I would be traded to the Raiders. He told me to come to Redskins Park and see him. They had actually worked out a deal the day before, but Coach Gibbs wanted to think it over.

When I went in to see him, Coach Gibbs was tied up in meetings. So I waited around until about one o'clock. Then he finally called me in and told me, "I've changed my mind. I think it's best for the team that you stay with us. I really believe somewhere down the line you're going to come in and play for us and help us win the Super Bowl."

I really thought it was a bunch of bullshit at the time. I mean I've been around so many coaches who try to motivate you by saying things like that. It seemed like it was one of those speeches that was supposed to make you feel good about not being traded. I was very disappointed. I thought I was going to the Raiders and would be their starting quarterback. To me, that was my best chance to get to play again. And suddenly, it was gone.

At the time, there was no way of knowing the Redskins were actually going to make it to the Super Bowl. Sure, we had a good chance. But it was early in the season, and every team had a chance to get to the Super Bowl. I looked at going to the Raiders as my chance. It was finally my chance to play again.

Of course, it turned out that the Redskins did make it to the Super Bowl, and I'm thankful I didn't miss out on that. I still think about it a lot, and I know Coach Gibbs thinks about how close we came to parting ways. If he had not turned down the trade, I probably never would have made it to the Super Bowl. We talk about it every once in a while. He mentioned it to me again last year when I was in his office.

"We were right here in this room when I told you that you were going to help us get to the Super Bowl," Coach Gibbs reminded me. "I just had a feeling it was going to work out that way."

Listening to him talk about it, you can tell Coach Gibbs really meant what he said. I'm sure he was being sincere. But at the time, I wanted to be traded so I could play. I didn't want to be told I was still going to be a backup.

By staying with the Redskins, I didn't think I would ever play. I really didn't. I also knew I wasn't going to get a pay raise as the backup quarterback. It didn't seem like a good situation for me. I thought I was stuck in the backseat and couldn't get out.

I'll never know what might have happened to the Raiders and to the Redskins if that trade had gone through. I do know it would have given me a chance to play right away, and I would have been playing for one of my favorite teams in the NFL. Of course, the Redskins are my favorite. I'm not sure how far they would have gone without me in 1987. I would never say they couldn't have made it to the Super Bowl without Doug Williams, that would be unfair to the other guys on the team. We didn't make it to the Super Bowl just because of me. It was a total team effort. Now if the Philadelphia Eagles made it to the Super Bowl, you'd have to say Randall Cunningham got them there. He's such a dominant player. They wouldn't even make the playoffs without Randall.

I thought I would spend 1987 watching from the sidelines again. Schroeder seemed to be more jittery about his position, though. He seemed to be looking over his shoulder. He realized that I had learned the system and was playing well. But he also knew he had the security of Joe Gibbs. Coach Gibbs does not pull his quarterbacks.

The worst thing that ever happened to Jay Schroeder was being picked for the Pro Bowl and getting a big contract. The Redskins gave him $900,000 a year. After that, his attitude went out the window. It ruined him. It was the worst possible thing that could happen to a young quarterback. First of all, I don't think he deserved to be in the Pro Bowl, but that wasn't up to me to determine. He had great team- mates who made him look good. After he played in the Pro Bowl, his ego ballooned, and it was already big to begin with. I don't think there was a hat in America that could have fit his head.

Schroeder took the attitude that "I'm the one who makes things click around here." He was extremely arrogant. Everyone noticed that he wanted to take control of things. He even wanted to be a coach. I remember he tried to tell Coach Gibbs what was right and what was wrong about our offense. You just don't do that. Coach Gibbs believes in what he does and has been doing it for a long time. He didn't want one of his players telling him what to do. Schroeder's attitude caused problems for everyone.

I think Coach Gibbs made the decision not to trade me because he realized that Schroeder might not be able to get the job done. Even though he had been to the Pro Bowl, he never really played that well. He had a good first half of the season in 1986, but he struggled in the second half. It was like a roller coaster. During a stretch of three games, he threw eleven interceptions. His success was just a matter of having some great receivers who were getting wide open for him. Jay Schroeder was never a great quarterback.

You have to play awfully bad as a starter for Coach Gibbs to pull you out of the lineup. But Schroeder was terrible in 1987. He just wasn't moving the team. He was missing his receivers and making lots of mistakes.

My first chance came in the first game of the season. We were playing Philadelphia, and Schroeder hurt his shoulder and had to come out. I came off the bench in the first quarter and led us to a 34-24 vic- tory. I think Coach Gibbs realized then that he had a capable backup who was ready to take over at any time.

But Schroeder came back for the next game and was the starter again. I had to come off the bench eight games later when we played Detroit. This time, Schroeder didn't have an injury. He just wasn't playing well and had to be taken out. I had another good game, and we won again.

In the last game of the regular season, we were playing at Minne- sota. It was the day after Christmas, and we had already clinched the NFC East championship. But we fell behind early, and Schroeder was having another bad game. Even though the game didn't mean anything as far as the playoffs, it's important that you play well down the stretch to keep your momentum going. So they put me into the game, and I played well again. I came in and hit Ricky Sanders going down the middle for a TD pass. Later, I hit him crossing over the middle, and he ran it in for a TD. We ended up beating the Vikings in overtime.

The Minnesota game was really important to me. It was a big, big game. It was crucial to the team that we played well. You don't want to be relaxing going into the playoffs. I felt like I lifted the team, and I could tell the other players felt that way. And they told me so. They were very comfortable and confident with me as the quarterback.

That's when Coach Gibbs finally decided he had to make a quarterback change. Everyone could see Schroeder wasn't playing to the level that we needed to make a run at the Super Bowl. So Coach Gibbs named me the starter for the playoffs.

It wasn't really a gamble making the change right before the playoffs started, because Joe Gibbs knew what I could do. I had come through for the team all three times I had got the chance in the 1987 season. And at that point, Coach Gibbs knew Schroeder couldn't do it. He had given Schroeder every possible chance, because he had committed to him as the starter and was paying him $900,000.

Coach Gibbs bent over backwards for Jay Schroeder. What made it bad was the players knew it. During the season, a lot of players came to me and said they couldn't understand why I wasn't the starter. It began after the Detroit game. An awful lot of players came to me. They were upset. They thought it was a black thing.

I just told them, ''I'm not worried about it, don't let it bother you. If that's what Coach Gibbs wants to do, that's what we'll do. It's fine with me.''

I didn't want to get caught up in a racial issue again. I didn't want to get wrapped up in it, because I had been in it enough. I had been fighting being a black quarterback all my life, and to make this a black issue would have been detrimental to the team. I think it could have split the team, so I didn't want to think that way.

I refused to believe it was a black thing. I respected Joe Gibbs too much to think that. But a lot of my teammates told me that's why I wasn't starting.

After I became the starter, Jay Schroeder wouldn't talk to me. He was pissed off because I took his position. He couldn't deal with it. When I had been the backup, I went about my business and tried to do whatever I could for the team. Sure, I wanted to play, but I accepted my role and tried to make the most of it. As soon as they benched him, Schroeder started acting like a spoiled little kid. All he did was sulk about it. The media tried to make a big deal about there being a feud between us, but we never had a run-in. There was never an incident between us. He just wouldn't talk to me, so I didn't bother to talk to him. That's all there was to it.

I was just glad to get a chance to be a starter in the NFL again. And there couldn't have been a better time to do it than in the playoffs. In my mind, this was the best chance I was ever going to get to lead a team to the Super Bowl. This was finally my shot.

It was also important to me to know that Coach Gibbs believed in me enough to name me the starter going into the playoffs. He thought if he was going to win it, he had to win it with me. I appreciated the confidence he had in me. It didn't matter to me that he had waited all season to make the move.

We couldn't have had a tougher way to open the playoffs. Even though we won our division, we had to go on the road and play at Chicago. The Bears had won the Super Bowl just two years before, and a lot of people thought they were going to make it back.

Not only did we have to play a great Bears team, but it was one of the coldest days of the year in Chicago. The temperature was 14 below with the wind chill. That's not the place for a country boy from Louisiana to be playing football.

When I went up there, I knew it was cold, too. But I also knew they were going to have to play in the cold. It was just a mental thing to me. Everybody said the Bears were used to it. That's bullshit. Nobody gets used to that kind of cold weather. If they were used to cold, they wouldn't have worn overcoats, and they wouldn't have gone to Notre Dame that week to practice inside the Gold Dome.

We were the ones who had practiced outside in Washington all week. There was about three feet of snow piled up on our Astroturf practice field and the wind whipped off it and cut into you. That made it feel like a deep freeze. Nobody is used to that kind of cold. Eskimos aren't used to it. So that was just talk. I made up my mind I wasn't going to let the weather affect anything I did.

The Bears had a good defense, but they weren't invincible. They had the strong people up front to make their defense work. Their front seven was really solid, and that made their defensive backs a lot better. They usually put great pressure on the quarterback. But we had a heck of an offensive line, and our offense was designed around not letting the quarterback get sacked. It was really a good matchup for us.

On the day before we played the Bears, we got a boost with the Minnesota Vikings beating San Francisco. The Vikings were the wild-card team so that meant if we could beat the Bears, the championship game would be in Washington. That would give us a tremendous advantage. So we told ourselves, "Win today, and we're going to the Super Bowl."

It didn't start well for us at all. We were down 14-0 in the first quarter. But we were a veteran team with a lot of confidence in ourselves. It didn't bother us to fall behind, and we didn't let the weather become a factor. We just stuck with our game plan, and things began to work for us.

Ricky Sanders just had a great day for us. In the second quarter, he made a sensational catch over the middle, getting hit hard as he caught the ball and holding on for the reception. That was the biggest play of the drive. George Rogers finished it off with a TD run.

We had another drive on our next possession. The Bears were in a defense that left our tight end, Clint Didier, one on one with a linebacker. It was no contest. Clint beat his man, and I hit him for our second TD to tie the score at 14-14.

That was definitely the turning point in the ballgame. It was freezing cold, and the Bears were two touchdowns ahead. Then all of a sudden, we're right back in it. We never let up. We didn't allow anything, being behind or the bad weather, affect what we set out to do. When we tied the game, we had all the momentum on our side. We believed we were going to win the second half.

Nobody did that much offensively in the second half. Both defenses were playing well. I did hit a couple passes to keep a drive alive, but it finally stalled. But Darrell Green later made a fantastic run on a punt return for a TD, and that won the game for us, 21-17.

By beating the Bears, we got to go home for the NFC championship game. We felt we had the 12th man on our side with the game being in D.C. We didn't think we could be beaten at home. Being that close to a Super Bowl was really a thrill. A lot of our older players had been to the Super Bowl, but I had never been. So I was like a kid in a candy store. I was so excited that week. We were rematched with the Vikings. Only this time, it was at RFK, and I didn't have to come off the bench.

Being in a championship game again was a great thrill for me. But being in a championship game at home was even more important. I felt RFK was going to give us the edge we needed to get to the Super Bowl.

The Vikings were a heck of a team at that point. They had killed the New Orleans Saints in the wild-card game, and then they beat up on the 49ers in San Francisco. And the 49ers had the best record in football.

Minnesota's defense was particularly good. They had Joey Browner, who is the best strong safety in football, and Floyd Peters, their defensive coordinator, put together a good scheme. They also had Chris Doleman and Keith Millard on the defensive line. As a defense, they were probably playing better than any other team in the league.

But we thought we had the kind of offense that could move the ball against anybody. It turned out the Hogs dominated the line. With Raleigh McKenzie blocking Millard like he owned him and Jake Jacoby doing a tremendous job on Doleman, we won the war up front.

But the Vikings still played well in the secondary. I think I completed something like 8 of 24 passes. It was a terrible day from a stats standpoint. But it was a great day for results. I had no sacks, no interceptions and two TD passes. I threw so many balls away that a lot of other guys probably would have eaten for sacks or thrown into coverage for an interception.

My philosophy has always been to throw the ball away rather than take a sack. And this game probably demonstrated better than any other how important that is. I did a lot of things to help the team, instead of hurting us by forcing passes.

I threw one TD to Kelvin Bryant and another to Gary Clark. We led all the way, but the Vikings stayed close and had a chance to tie us late in the game and force overtime. We were leading 17-10, and they drove to our 5-yard line. On fourth-and-goal, Wade Wilson threw a pass to Darrin Nelson in the end zone, but Darrell Green broke it up to save the game.

After three tries, I had finally won a championship game. I didn't get all that emotional. I like to keep my feelings to myself for the most part. I was very elated to be going to the Super Bowl, though. A lot of people ask me what's the most important game I've ever played in, and they expect me to say the Super Bowl. But I always say the Minnesota game, because that's the one that got me there. We were headed to San Diego for Super Bowl XXII. The Denver Broncos had won the AFC championship game and were heavy favorites to beat us.

As soon as they could, the media colored me up quickly. In the press conference after the championship game, they didn't waste a minute going after me. All they wanted to ask was what's it like to be the first black quarterback to go to the Super Bowl? That was the line of questioning by everyone who tried to interview me. A lot of them tried to make it a negative thing. They wanted me to say something controversial.

My answer was always, "I'm not a black quarterback. I'm the Washington Redskins' quarterback."

That wasn't what they were looking for, so they'd ask the same stupid question in a different way. They wanted to get me started on how the NFL hasn't given black quarterbacks a fair chance. I didn't need to say that, because that's obvious. I knew how to handle those kind of questions. I had heard them a million times.

What I did was play away from the controversial questions. I knew it was going to happen, but I still didn't want to have to deal with it. I wanted to be able to focus on the game. I had been dealing with black quarterback questions all of my life, and I didn't want to even think about it at that time.

It took about a day for it to sink in that I was actually going to play in the Super Bowl. I thought about all the things that I had been through to get that far, all the trouble that I had to overcome, all the opportunities that I didn't get because I was black, and the way they treated me at Tampa. A lot of those things went through my mind. And then I began to realize that everything I had worked for had come true. I was in the Super Bowl.

It was a very exciting time for me, and I was all by myself in my apartment in Virginia. At the time when I really needed someone to be with me, Lisa wasn't there. She was at home with her momma. So it's not like she played a role in helping me succeed. We had been talking off and on ever since she left me, and that week, she called me or I called her. I really don't remember who called who. We started discussing things and got on the subject of the Super Bowl. And I think I asked her if she was coming to the game.

She said right away, "Sure, I want to come."

Well, I knew she wasn't going to miss the party. That was just the kind of thing Lisa lived for, and there was no way she was going to stay away from San Diego. I was open to a lot of things, because I still wanted to make the marriage work. After all, I had married Lisa, so I felt I should try to work things out. There were still some feelings there. At the same time, I had made it that far without Lisa, and I knew I didn't have to have her. I knew I could make it on my own.

14

Super Week

It was as cold as the dickens in Washington, so we were ecstatic about the prospects of going to San Diego for the Super Bowl. During our week of practice at Redskins Park, we had snow piled up on the sides of the field. It was so cold that it felt like we were back in Chicago.

Even though we took off Monday and Tuesday after winning the NFC title, it was business as usual for Joe Gibbs. Playing in the Super Bowl just gave him one extra week to prepare. And he took advantage of that extra time to put in more work on the game plan. His theory was that he gave us a couple days off, but he expected us to work harder than ever. Joe is the Smith and Barney type of coach. He does things the old-fashioned way.

Coach Gibbs knows how to motivate you and how to get you ready for that particular opponent. He tells you the incentives of winning and what the game is all about. Everything he does is very thorough and I think his attitude extends over to the players. We always wanted to do everything we could to prepare. We were always ready to play, but our focus was to make it to the playoffs and then turn it up a notch once we got there. Joe Gibbs instilled that in us.

Practicing that week wasn't really like work for us. When you're in the Super Bowl, you want to do everything you can to get ready.

This was for all the marbles, and we didn't want to waste any chance to get better. This was it. The top of the hill. They don't get any bigger than this. And there were plenty of us who had never made it this far. So this was really exciting for us.

I'm not an emotional person. I kept my cool through the whole two weeks. I always acted like I belonged there. Daddy always told me that if you've never been somewhere, just act like you belong there. And that's what I did.

The city of Washington was going crazy over the Redskins. They already were great fans, and once we made it to the Super Bowl, that's all they wanted to talk about. When the Redskins win, the whole city of Washington wins. It's an incredible place to play football. You're somebody if you play for the Washington Redskins. I really didn't get involved in the Super Bowl hoopla, because I didn't go into the city that much. I try to stay away from crowds most of the time and out of the limelight.

That week, I spent most of my off time at the apartment talking to family and friends on the phone. I got a lot of calls. Everyone wanted to get tickets for the game. Of course, I wanted my family to be there, and I wanted to help them with the arrangements. I paid for twenty-two of them to go to the game. I took care of it all. Everything. From plane tickets to hotel rooms to game tickets. What I did was figure out how much I'd be making in the playoffs, and I spent it all on my family. Naturally, Ashley was going to be there. All of my brothers and sisters came except Josephine, who was sick. M'Dear made the trip, too, but Daddy decided not to come. He probably could have come. He just never liked to travel after he started using a wheelchair.

The team flew into San Diego on Sunday, a week before the game. There was a lot of fanfare, media coverage and things like that. But it wasn't anything we weren't used to. It was a relief to get out of the cold weather. For us, going to a warm climate like San Diego was a great reward for what we had done that season. We had worked hard all year to get to the Super Bowl, and now we could enjoy it.

The media rush was harder on me than the other guys on the team. Most of them could go out on the town and just enjoy themselves. We were staying at the San Diego Marriott, and whenever I came downstairs, the media people were always trying to get me for interviews or the fans were lined up for autographs. There was no way to relax.

Instead of getting caught up in the crowd, I just stayed in my room by myself and did a lot of thinking, I didn't even go out to eat. While everyone else was having fun in San Diego, I ordered a lot of room service and watched a lot of TV.

Lisa didn't get there until Friday. You might think that would distract me, but it didn't. Being separated from her didn't distract me, so having her back wasn't going to distract me, either. I wasn't going to let anything or anyone get in the way of preparing for this game.

All that week, my mission was not to be disturbed no matter who was there. Not Lisa. Not Ashley and M'Dear. Not my brothers and sisters. Not the media. Not the fans. And certainly not John Elway and the Broncos.

The media was really annoying, but I didn't let them get me upset. They were swarming around me like flies on stink. I've never seen so many TV cameras and tape recorders. They were all desperate to get a story. It's such a wild situation that the media pack is called the zoo. I think it's more like the jungle. There's just mobs of media. Everybody who's somebody in the business is there asking all sorts of questions. You name it, they asked it. Sometimes, I thought I should have tape-recorded their questions.

Every morning, there was an hour-long interview period for the players. I didn't go for the whole time, because you don't need to spend a whole hour answering questions. There's only so many things you can say. So I went there for about a half hour every day. I would be at one station, and the reporters would keep coming and coming. I lost count of how many people I talked to each day.

When reporters would track me down later in the day, I wouldn't give any interviews. I'd just tell them that they had to catch me during the interview session. That's why they set it up that way.

I remember this one radio lady who was really a nuisance. I had never seen her before and had no idea who she was. She kept bugging me about who was the best quarterback in the Super Bowl. Of course, she wanted me to say that I was. But I wouldn't play her game.

"What do you think about Elway?" she asked.

"Ma'am, I'm not here to talk about John Elway. I'm not playing Elway."

"Well, do you think you're better than Elway?"

This went on and on. She kept asking these stupid questions, thinking I would fall into her trap. Finally, I just stared her in the eye and said, "Read my lips. I am not comparing myself to Elway. Thank you."

I could have kicked her ass. She was such a pain. And there were plenty of others just like her. It never stopped all week. No matter what I said, they continued to ask the same dumb questions.

For the most part, of course, they wanted to know how I felt about being the first black quarterback in the Super Bowl. Then they'd ask if I thought this would create more opportunities for black quarterbacks, if this would open the door for more blacks to play the position, and if the NFL owners would be more open to playing black quarterbacks.

When it was all over with, I honestly believe the media learned to respect me. I think they eventually began to appreciate the way I handled all those questions before the game and had to go through it all over again after the game. I answered their questions politely. I remained humble, and I went about my business.

Our practices were great all week. We worked out at some small college in San Diego. The weather was warm and sunny, and we were really having fun. But the intensity was there, too. Based on the way we had prepared, I figured we were going to win the game.

You could feel the spirit on the team. Everyone was hustling and working so hard. But at the same time, the coaches were relaxed, and the players were relaxed. We had fun that week, and anytime you're enjoying yourself, you do a better job than if you're unhappy. I think a lot of it had to do with leaving that freezing weather in Washington and getting into the sixty-five degree weather in San Diego. Our bones and our muscles felt better so it was easy to get loose. I don't think we could have been any more ready to play a game.

Everything seemed to go right for us during the week. Even with so many things going on around us, Coach Gibbs made sure we remained focused on the game. It would have been easy to have our minds on the festivities. But we never did. We weren't there for the party. The party could come after the game. And that's what we did. The team party was planned for Sunday night, after we completed our mission on Sunday afternoon.

In any football game, you have to win the war up front. We felt our offensive line was a lot stronger than their defensive line. The Broncos were strictly a finesse defense. The next year they tried to become more of an attack defense, but when we played them, they were definitely finesse. As long as the game was close, we felt we would wear them down and beat them.

Our offensive game plan was perfect to beat the Broncos. Coach Gibbs does not believe in just going right at somebody. He's got a system of coming up with the right plays to take advantage of what the defense gives up. We didn't go into the Super Bowl thinking we were going to run against them or we were going to throw the football. What we tried to do was mix everything into our plan. Against the Broncos, we became a power finesse offense. We had finesse with our passing game and power with our running game. We had everything we needed to beat Denver.

Coach Gibbs' goal is always to score at least twenty-one points. He feels if his offense gets twenty-one, his defense will hold the opponent to less than that, and it will be a victory. We felt we were going to score twenty-one against the Broncos. We were confident of that. Obviously, the Broncos did some things well on defense or they wouldn't have made it to the Super Bowl. They blitzed linebackers and moved people around to get them in position to make big plays. What we had to do was find out what they were going to do as far as tricks on defense. Then we had to power them out of those positions. We knew we had to play well to beat them. But we expected to play well.

I could have pulled a Joe Namath, if I was that type of individual. It would have been easy to predict a victory over the Broncos. I felt so good about our team.

During the whole week, I went out to eat just once. I wouldn't have gone that time, but Jimmy Giles was in town and came to get me. We went to a seafood restaurant by the water. It was a nice, quiet place, and nobody bothered us. We ate dinner and sat there talking about old times. We reminisced about Tampa Bay, and there were some good stories to tell.

Jimmy was really happy for me. And if he had been in the Super Bowl, I would have been there to watch him and I would have been glad for him. I think I've got a lot of Jimmy Giles in me. Jimmy came from a family that's very similar to mine. He had a hard-working mom and dad. There were lots of kids in the family, so they struggled. He grew up in Mississippi, so it was just about like what I had to deal with in Zachary. Then he went to a small black school, Alcorn State. Being from the same background, we have the same kind of values. We never had much while we were growing up, so we really value and treasure what we have now. We don't throw our money away. We're not extravagant. Success hasn't changed the type of individuals we are.

We often talk about how the big schools and the big money can affect some players. A lot of the guys who go to the large universities really lose sight of what's going on. They give you so much at those places. If you can play the game, they'll take care of you, and it spoils you. We're fortunate that we didn't go through that. Jimmy and I will always appreciate what we have, because it took so much to get it.

My family came to town on Thursday. There were three days to go before the game, and that's when things could have gotten hectic. But I didn't let it get out of hand. They were all staying in the Marriott, too, but I didn't spend that much time with them. They went out on the town. I made sure they had plenty to keep themselves busy.

One day, I rented a limousine, so they could go to Mexico. The rest of the time, they went sightseeing around San Diego and enjoyed some of the events that were planned for the Super Bowl. They had a great time, and I was alone like I wanted to be. Coach Robinson was there for several days, and I never did see him until after the game.

Mainly, I spent my time studying the play book. I thought a lot about the significance of what was about to happen. I never really felt the pressure that I was supposed to feel. I look at pressure as something you put on yourself or allow people to put on you. And I refused to put myself in a pressure situation. What people were writing in the newspaper and saying on TV didn't mean anything to me. I looked at things differently. I saw it from my standpoint.

I didn't pay any attention to the black-white issue. I didn't believe it when people said we didn't have a chance to win the game. It didn't matter to me what anyone else thought about me or my team. I made sure I kept my mind on the game and on winning. By the end of the week, I just wanted to play the game and get it over with. As Coach Robinson would say, "Let the peace dove fly out the window."

We had our final practice on Saturday morning. There wasn't much left to work on. Everyone was ready to play, and we had another super practice. We were really sharp. I think everyone felt we had the edge that we needed to win the Super Bowl.

After practice, there was a barbecue for the team. I was getting something to eat, and that's when my tooth started aching.

I went to see our team dentist, Dr. Barry Rudolph, hoping he could give me something to make it stop hurting. But after a quick look at the tooth, we were off to a dental office. When he told me that I needed a root canal, my Super Bowl fun was over. I was in pain the rest of the day.

Fortunately, Dr. Rudolph must be some kind of dentist, because I was fine by the next morning. I was feeling great on Super Sunday and couldn't wait to get to the game.

Winning the Super Bowl the way we did, 42-10, was obviously a tremendous thrill. We had accomplished our mission. We were the world champions. That night, we got our party.

I was the only Redskins player who didn't go to the party. My knee, which I injured in the first quarter, was killing me. The novocaine shot I took at halftime had worn off, so I went up to my room and took some pain pills. All my family was with me. We stayed up talking about the game and all the excitement of winning the Super Bowl.

Even when I woke up the next morning, I was still in excruciating pain. My knee was all swollen up and stiff, I could hardly walk and I had trouble getting dressed.

Despite that, it was starting to sink in that we had actually won the Super Bowl. I began to realize what I had accomplished. It was very satisfying to have performed so well in a Super Bowl. There were a lot of people out there who wanted to see Doug Williams fall flat on his face. I'm sure a lot of people were shocked the way it turned out.

It was a great feeling. Mentally, I was at a point that I didn't care if I ever threw another football. I had been there, and that's what it's all about.

15

The Pay Back

Growing up, I never met a professional athlete. I never saw a pro football game until I played in one. So once I became a pro, I wanted to be accessible to the kids. I wanted to give back to the community, give back to the young people and be a positive influence on their lives.

I always try to be the type of person that kids will look up to and say, "I want to grow up and be like Doug Williams. I want to do the things that Doug does." Hopefully, they'll be in a situation some day that they will be able to give something back.

In Washington, there are so many murders and so much drugs, and unfortunately, the young people are involved in a lot of it. I feel compelled to do something to help the situation. It hurts me to see the kids in that city ruining their lives.

Being the Super Bowl MVP is kind of like my monument in D.C. People tend to put me on a pedestal. Sometimes I hate being in that position. But I realize it's a good opportunity to help those young people. They need someone positive to look up to, and I'm that type of person for them. I think by being visible to the kids, going to their schools, talking to them on the streets, I can make a difference. I can help them overcome some of their problems. I want them to say to themselves, "If Doug Williams did it, I can do it."

I've always liked kids and tried to get involved with helping them wherever I've been. At Grambling, the athletes worked with the kids in what's called the National Youth Sports Program. They'd bring in kids from the area and get them involved in different sports. Volleyball, badminton, football, basketball, baseball and all the others. What it did was give the kids something constructive to do in the summer time. It got them active in sports and kept them out of trouble. And there were lectures, so we'd get a chance to teach them something. Even as a college player, I understood the importance of working with kids.

After the Super Bowl, I thought it was a good time to start something on a large scale. Herb Nelson, who went to school with me at Grambling, suggested starting a Doug Williams fan club. I didn't like that idea. I didn't think it was right for me to have a fan club. That's too much of a personal thing. I've always been a team player, and I didn't want to promote myself with a fan club. Also, where does the money go in a fan club? I guess it would go to me, and I wasn't looking for anything like that. I wanted to give something back. I didn't need people giving me anything.

I told Herb that I would be willing to start a non-profit foundation. So we got together with a couple of other Grambling alumni, Suzanne Mayo and Leo Givs, and started hammering this thing out. It got bigger and bigger, because the concept was to go out and help the kids. We wanted to stress the importance of staying in school and keeping away from drugs and making something of your life. Then we started talking to people about it. So many became interested in it, because there was such a great need for something like this in Washington. Plus, a lot of people became involved because of Doug Williams. So we got it off the ground. We decided to call it the Doug Williams Foundation.

I really wanted to contribute something to Washington. I had been fortunate enough to have been there for two years, and the city had been so good to me. I felt I had been adopted by the area. They treated me like I belonged there. After that, I wanted to do something to say, ''Thank you for giving me this opportunity. I want to spend my time giving something back to you.''

Our main goal was to go into the community and deal with the kids on a personal basis. We wanted to take a hands-on approach to it.

I wanted to be right there in front of the kids, where they co
to me and get to know what I was all about and I could influer
I didn't want to be a figurehead. This wasn't going to be on€
deals that Doug Williams put his name on the foundation, b
back and lets someone else do all the work. I wanted to be o
the kids, to visit the schools, to go to the functions that th
on and to have lots of contact with them.

I thought it was important for the young people to be a
to me and ask, "Doug Williams, did you go to class?" oi "Doug
Williams, do you do drugs?" I wanted to be out there doing something. I felt I should be a driving force in the area and give those kids a
positive outlook in their lives. At the time, I thought I really had
something important to share with them, because I had been through
so many things and I wanted to let them know that they could overcome all the obstacles and problems they were facing.

Suzanne Mayo became the executive director of the foundation,
and we've got about twelve people working on the staff. The office is
located on K Street in downtown D.C. We've got a lot of programs, so
we need a pretty big staff to run it.

In our "Stay in School" program, we go right to the schools and
talk to the students about the importance of education and how to
avoid drugs. We've also got a "Life Skills Training" program in which
we teach everyday skills like setting up a checking account, how to
write a check, what to do on a job interview and basic things like writing a letter. Then we've got what we call TREP, which stands for
Train and Retrain an Experienced Person. What we do is take someone who has some experience in a certain area and retrain them for
another area, such as computers. There's also a "Success Through
Sports" program in which we go into the community and get the kids
involved in sports. But we also teach them how to function in society
and how to deal with other people, and mix it in with being a good
sportsman.

When I go to the schools, none of the kids knows that I'm coming. I walk in unannounced. If they knew I was coming, they would tell
their parents and friends and there would be a big crowd. That's not
what we want. We want to deal with the kids.

It's amazing the kind of reactions I get. That's the thrill for me.
The kids are the thrill. They think it's just going to be some kind of

assembly. Then they see Doug Williams walk in, and they go crazy. You're dealing with kids who don't get a chance to get that close to a professional athlete. The only exposure they get with pro athletes is what they see on TV. It's really exciting to the young kids. Their little eyes start popping open and you hear the "oohs and aahs." I guess it's hard for them to believe I'm real, because they only see me on TV. It's a great feeling to see the kids respond like that. Even the teachers get excited. Most of them are diehard fans, and they don't get to see any of the Redskins. And now all of a sudden, I'm walking right down the halls of their school.

Tuesday was my day off with the Redskins, so every Tuesday I went out to the schools. I usually visited two or three schools a day. I went to junior high and high schools. I even visited elementary schools for the fourth, fifth and sixth graders.

The only thing you can do is give them the information in a way that you hope makes an impact. You can't be out there walking the streets with them. They're going to have to make up their own minds. But you can help them make the right decisions.

I always use examples of the consequences of drug abuse. I talk about what it has done to Dexter Manley and Lawrence Taylor and people like that. I tell them what happened to some of the guys I played with at Tampa Bay. I explain to them what drugs do for you, what they can't do for you, and what they will make you do. To me, that's the best prevention you can have.

In Dexter's case, the biggest problem was he didn't have a good role model. My father was always there for his kids. He would tell us what we should and shouldn't do and let us know he wouldn't help us if we got in trouble with drugs. We were going to jail if that happened. You've got to have someone reinforce that to you as a youngster. I don't think Dexter had that. And I think going to a big college like Oklahoma State and getting everything he wanted didn't help. He came out and said he couldn't read. Well, how did he get through high school and college? They just let him play football and kept him eligible. That didn't help Dexter with his problems. It just made it worse by facilitating it for him.

Then Dexter went into the pros and had some success. How you handle success is an individual thing, and I don't think Dexter handled it as well as he could have. He may have let success go to his head.

And when you do that, you've always got people who want to be your friend, who are always going to come up to you and offer you stuff that you don't need. That's what those kind of friends do. I know a lot of people say drug abuse is a sickness and it's hard to stay away from it. But I find it hard to believe that if you know you're going to be drug tested two or three times a week, you would still go back to it. I would think that would be enough of a deterent. But it wasn't with Dexter. I can't say I feel sorry for Dexter. I do feel sorry for Dexter's family. In the long run, the kids are the ones who will suffer most.

I think Dexter will come back to football. But the important thing is will he straigthen out his life? Coming back to the game is one thing. But coming back all the way to a life of order is another. And that's what I'm hoping for, that Dexter can take care of Dexter. I want to see Dexter get himself on the right track for the rest of his life, not just for a couple of years, so he can finish his football career.

Even though I talk about the Dexters and Lawrence Taylors of football, I don't think that drug abuse is more prevalent in professional sports than any other facet of society. Drugs are a problem with people. It just so happens that you've got professional athletes who are people. We're in the high visibility category. When an L.T. or Dexter gets in trouble with drugs, the cameras are rolling. Whereas if Joe Blow and Mary Doe do the same thing, nobody knows about it. The media puts us in a position where we're different than other people. It shouldn't be that way. We're just like any other red-blooded American. We bleed when we get cut, and we cry when we get hurt. But being so visible, we get in trouble, and it's all over CNN. We've got about 1,600 pro football players, and you think about the small number that actually has been caught using drugs. The percentage is small. It's probably smaller than doctors and lawyers and politicians. But we're in the spotlight, and people are going to make an example of us.

I tell the kids my way of staying away from drugs is making up my mind I don't need them. I don't need anything to get me high. I have a natural high. I don't smoke. I don't drink. A lot of it has to do with your will. It all comes down to wanting to be a leader, not a follower. I want to be a leader.

You can't last very long in anything if you're a follower. You've got to stand up for yourself and when you do that, you are a leader. Plus, I believe in obeying the law. It's illegal to use drugs, and I'm not going to break the law. I tell the kids about my father telling us if you get caught with drugs, you're going to jail. That's all that drugs will do for you. Put you in jail and ruin your life.

The real answer to stopping the drug problem lies on Capitol Hill. You've got to stop the big-time smugglers. The local guys are getting put in jail all the time, but as soon as you put one in jail, you've got another one coming up to take his place. Our country has to stop the stuff from getting here. The supply has to be shut off. If the politicians really crack down on the big-time smugglers, maybe one day they'll run out of drugs and we won't have a drug problem. But as long as there's a supply, people are going to use drugs.

You can sit there and tell a kid not to do something, but he's not necessarily going to listen to you. When you tell kids not to do something, they just get curious as to why. But if you tell them the why, if you explain to them how it can result in death or suicide or ruining your life, it will help them understand that those are the consequences.

Another thing we do to get our message across is bring a rap group with us to the schools. It's made up of some high school students and a little boy. What they do is sing a song called "Don't Take That Crack, Brother." It's really a good song, and I think it's important to have young people involved in the presentation. They're expressing their feelings about drugs to other students. I think it really helps to have some of their own peer group, their age and even younger, singing this song about the dangers of crack. And they do it with a lot of feeling.

The kids really listen to me. They listen to everything I tell them. I visited two high schools in New York last January. These schools were huge with about 2,500 or 3,000 students. Here I am a country boy from Zachary, Louisiana, and I'm talking to kids from New York City. They probably could tell me more about drugs than I could even imagine. But because of who I am, they listened. I talked about where I grew up and how I grew up and the things I had to overcome. And I talked about the things that young kids have to face today and how they have to be a leader and make decisions for themselves and think for themselves and stay away from people who want to lead them astray. And when I was getting ready to leave, some of the teachers told me that they could tell the students really got a lot out of it. They had listened to everything I said.

Getting the foundation started has been much more difficult than

I anticipated. It's been awfully, awfully hard to raise the money that we need to run our organization. Many of the people who originally said they were going to contribute have not come through for us. I'm talking about big businesses and corporations. Corporate America wants people to think they're concerned, but when it comes time to give some money, it's a different story. It's really tough to get their cooperation. I've found out a lot of people only donate when a friend or associate calls them and says, "Why don't you give something to this charity." So much of what these corporations say they're going to do is just talk. They really don't do it.

It's been a struggle, but we've kept afloat and we're headed in the right direction. We're doing everything we can to make this work. I've put about $180,000 of my own money into it—and it's money well spent. The city has helped by giving us some grants. So the foundation is operating, and it's doing things to help the kids. The important thing is the people working for the foundation believe in what we're doing. And I believe in what we're doing.

Spending the day with those kids is a tremendous feeling. To me, it's the best feeling anyone could possibly have. I think it's something every athlete should want to experience. When you walk into a school and see that young kid who wants to be like you and wants to accomplish some of the things that you've achieved, it makes it all worthwhile. I totally enjoy going to the schools. You know you're doing something meaningful.

Sometimes on Tuesdays I wanted to be soaking in a whirlpool all day because I was still aching from the game. At other times, I wanted to make some trips out of town. I could have left Monday night and gone somewhere for a couple of days. I could have done a lot of other things on my off days—but I didn't. My commitment is to the kids, and I'm going to be there for them.

I've always wanted to help people. I think it's something that just comes naturally. I don't think it's something you can learn, it's something that grows in you over time. I've always loved kids, and I thought helping them was a good way to get involved in the community. Kids are so much fun to be around. When I'm out signing autographs, if I see older people walk up and push the kids out of the way, I act like I don't even see them. I just sign for everyone else and ignore them. If they say, "Doug, Doug, sign my shirt," I tell them, "I know you're there, but you didn't pay any attention to these kids when you pushed your way up here.'' Kids are important to me, and I want them to be important to everyone else, too.

Anyone who has been successful in life should try to do things for others. I think it's almost an obligation. So what I do shouldn't be all that big of a deal. It's strange when a newspaper like the *Washington Post,* one of the foremost papers in the country, writes that I'm a folk hero in Washington. At the same time, it does make you feel good. It shows you have accomplished something in life and still you've given back to the community. It's not like I accomplished something and bottled it up for my own use and said, ''The heck with everybody else.''

Believe me, I don't go out to the schools and I don't put my money into the foundation so that I can get praised by the media. I've never done anything in my life for the media's sake. I'm not looking to impress anyone or get paid back. I get paid back every time I get together with those kids. And hopefully I'm making a difference. I'm always going to do these things, because I believe in it. I think your time is so much more important than any money you could give. The children want to see you in person, and they want to hear what you've got to say. And they listen when you take the time to come see them.

Hardly a day goes by that I don't get a call from some organization that wants me to come speak. Most of them aren't going to pay anything, either. I tell them, ''I understand. I'm not interested in being paid. I want to help.'' Usually, I'm able to find a way to work it into my schedule. I hate to turn anyone down, because most likely that means the kids will be disappointed. They're the ones who will miss out.

There are such great needs in Washington. The president is right there in the nation's capital. Drug czar William Bennett is right there in D.C. But they can't even seem to get a handle on the problems going on in the city. If the politicians can't figure a way to improve things, I don't know what can be done. All anyone can do is try to reach as many of the children as they can, and that's what the foundation does.

It didn't help any of us in D.C. when Mayor Marion Barry got into trouble with drugs. Since Barry is such a prominent leader in the city, it's a terrible shame that he let himself get into that situation. It really hurts what our foundation and other programs are trying to accomplish. It's really a bad example for the kids, and the D.C. youth already have such a serious problem with drugs. Here's a man that always spoke out strongly about the dangers of crack, and then the kids hear that he's been charged with possession and use of crack. It's a tough pill to swallow. It did a lot of harm.

Dexter's problems last season made it tougher for us, too. That may have been more damaging than Mayor Barry, because a lot of the kids get the impression that drug use is rampant among pro athletes. So what I have to do is convince them that's not the case. I tell them about Dexter's situation, but I make it clear that he's one of the exceptions. All pro athletes are not drug heads. The kids just have to take my word on that.

These kids know what's going on in the world. They've been asking me about Dexter for months. And I know they'll be asking about Mayor Barry now. I don't try to hide anything from them. I give them all the information I have, because they know if you're holding back. Dexter and the mayor are just two examples of the consequences of drugs. I believe that's what the kids need to hear. That's what will make the greatest impact on them.

I think that I will always have a place in Washington's heart, because I know D.C. will always have a place in my heart. There are so many people in that city who have been instrumental in my being where I am today and the success I've had. I won't ever forget what they've done for me and what they've meant to me. Those people are my Washington, D.C.

It will be hard for me not to keep a home in the D.C. area. If I'm coaching, I'll be able to get back during the offseason. If I'm doing something else, I'll probably be able to spend more time in Washington. I believe that I'll always have a job to do there. And I'll always feel wanted in D.C.

There are also needs to be met in my hometown. Even though the little town of Zachary doesn't have the drug troubles that D.C. has, there's still a problem there and throughout the Baton Rouge area. Drugs are wherever people are. The kids in that area have other problems that I might be able to help them with, too.

One thing that I've been able to do is reach some children through an annual football clinic that I hold in Baton Rouge. What I really like about the clinic is that it's something I started before I went to the Super Bowl and became well known to a lot of people.

The clinic has been going for eight years. The funny thing is I wasn't that big on clinics before I started this one. I had participated in quite a few and didn't really like it too much. The Delta Sigma Theta sorority actually suggested the idea for a clinic. Janice was a Delta, and they thought it would be a good service to the community. So I agreed to do it.

It's something I've enjoyed every year. We only have the kids for about three hours, so you have to cover as much as you can in a hurry. We try to teach them something about football and something about life. What we try to do is instill in the kids the importance of getting an education, the importance of staying away from drugs and the importance of being a good person.

The players and coaches talk about the things they had to do to get where they are. It takes great sacrifices. You just don't come out of your mother's womb with a football in your hand and go right to the NFL. They all faced tremendous challenges along the way. They all had to go to school. They had to go through the same routine of attending class and doing homework. I think we're able to get the message across to the kids. When I'm out in the community, some of the kids come up to me and say, "I was at the clinic last year and I remember what you told me."

I think the main thing is the kids appreciate you taking time to spend with them. It makes an impact when you're out there trying to help them, no matter what you're talking about.

Every year I've been able to get a couple teammates or friends to come to the clinic. We don't get any of the big names, because we can't afford to pay anything. It's all strictly on a volunteer basis. Last year, I got two of my teammates from the Redskins, Ravin Caldwell and Eric Yarber. This year it was Jimmy Giles. These guys come because they want to share something with the kids.

LSU and Southern also help us out by sending some of their coaches. They've been very eager to help us. So we're able to put together a pretty good group of coaches. We usually have 300 to 350 kids, and what we do is rotate them from station to station teaching just the basics of each position. We're out on the field for a couple hours, and then we take time to talk to them. It's really worked well, but of course, you'd always like to get more kids involved.

Now that my playing days may be over, I want to become even

more active in the community. I've talked to some of my friends at home about setting up some type of organization to help our community grow and prosper and to work with the kids. It would be something along the lines of a civic club. We've gotten together and discussed doing it. I think it should be a community organization open to men and women. We need to set something like that up to take care of the needy people. We could bring them food and clothing when they need it. We could have drives to pick up clothing from families and businesses that normally might just throw it away. There are a lot of things you can do to help out. I try to think about those who don't have much. That's what a civic organization should be concerned with.

We also need a community center, gymnasium or park for the kids. Then we could set up activities to get them off the streets and get them involved with sports. When you've got the kids interested in sports, then you can talk to them about other things.

The church that I attend, Greater Philadelphia Baptist Church, is very active in helping the needy. They give out food baskets during the holidays and do quite a few other things like that. We have about 300 members. But you can always do more.

Once I stop playing football, I'm going to have time to be active in things like that. I want to do all that I can and make a difference.

I want the kids to have a vision that going down the street of drugs and dropping out of school is the wrong way. I want them to realize the price you pay to go down the right way is hard work and dedication. You have to have the will to go the right way. It's very easy to go the wrong way—that's a smooth road. But going the right way is always a little rocky, a little tough at times, but you've got to weather the storm.

My hope is the kids will have the ambition to want to excel and put out the effort to succeed. One thing I've always found to be true is you must work hard, nobody is going to give it to you. Unless you're born with a silver spoon in your mouth, you're going to have to work for everything, and you're going to have to suffer. But when you get what you want, it's going to be awfully good.

For me to get to the Super Bowl, I had to overcome an awful lot of things. Pain from injuries. Pain from emotional stress. But in the end, it was all worthwhile. You appreciate it more when you've worked for it. When I come home at night, I can enjoy my house because it's my house and I worked for it. Nobody gave it to me.

I hope the kids will feel the same way. I hope they'll want to go to college and get a good job. I hope they'll want to work hard for all of that. Then they'll be able to buy a house of their own or a car of their own. And they can say, "That's my house. My parents didn't give it to me. I bought it myself." It's a great feeling to know you earned something. It really means something when you can say to yourself, "I did it." That's the hope I have for the kids of this world.

16

More Adversity

It looked like 1988 was going to be a great year for me. We had just won the Super Bowl. I was the Super Bowl MVP. Everyone was talking about how much money Doug Williams was going to make on endorsements and appearances and things like that. They said Phil Simms made about $2 million, and I could make that much or more. But I didn't really listen to them.

When it came down to actually signing me for these big deals, I didn't get any calls from the major corporations. None. Not a single company wanted me for a national advertising campaign.

The only thing close was Coca-Cola, but they didn't want me for national ads. They were going to pay me to represent them at functions held at black colleges. They offered to pay me $375,000 for three years, but I had to make about thirty appearances. No ads. Just on the run every weekend traveling all the time. I never would have had any time to myself. Every time a black college had a banquet, Coca-Cola was going to ship me out there. That's the only reason they contacted me. It wasn't going to be like Joe Montana, Dr. J, Dominique Wilkins or Michael Jordan drinking a Coke on a TV commercial.

It didn't really surprise me. After going through the things I've been through in my life, I understand how things work. I know that Doug Williams, the black quarterback, wasn't what Corporate America wanted. They weren't ready for that. Everybody was geared up for John Elway to win the Super Bowl and shoot all the commercials. When we won the Super Bowl and I was named MVP, it kind of drove a stake through their hearts.

I was not what they wanted to represent their corporations. That's one thing I never had a problem with. If Corporate America didn't want me, I didn't want them. I took the approach that I never had the endorsements, so I wasn't going to let it bother me that I didn't get them. If I had gotten them, that would have been nice. But I wasn't going to let it get to me.

The irony of the Coca-Cola deal was both of the people I was dealing with were black. I guess to them it was a good deal to offer me. Their job is to make sure the black colleges are covered. They probably thought they were giving me a great opportunity. But they were just talking about the black segment of Coca-Cola's marketing. They didn't want Doug Williams for the national ads.

I got a few small contracts, but one was with Supreme Beauty, a black company owned by Johnson Publishing Company that puts out *Jet* and *Ebony*. Another one was Kuppenheimer men's suits. And the only other one was Van Grack, a new sports attire business. I own part of that company, so I might be the only athlete who owns a line of sports apparel. Our company puts out apparel that's highly fashionable. My job is to make sure other pro athletes are aware of our company. I supply them with warmup suits or shoes to let them know what our company is all about.

After all the talk about the millions I'd be making, I was lucky to clear $200,000 from endorsements. I guess I didn't have the right hair style for the national advertisers.

At that time, I was also in line for a pay raise with the Redskins. That's something I didn't worry about, because I believed the Redskins were the type of organization that takes care of its players. I already had a contract through the 1988 season, but I felt strongly that the organization would give me a better deal.

The media made a big deal out of it, but I was never concerned. They kept asking, "When are you going to get the new contract? When? When? When?"

I just told them, "I've got a job to do and you've got a job to do. Don't worry about my job. When the Redskins think it's time to give me a new contract, they'll do it."

After the Super Bowl, Bobby Beathard told me that Jack Kent Cooke was going to deal with me. Coach Gibbs said the same thing to me. That's all I needed to hear. I felt they would treat me fairly. I was going to get what any other top starter in the league was making. They told me I was going to be the starter, so I knew I would get at least what Jay Schroeder had been paid in 1987. That was $900,000, so anything in that range would have been double my current salary. At that time, they didn't deal with me as a black quarterback. They treated me just like anyone else.

Right after our first preseason game, Mr. Cooke called me into his office and told me what he had planned. He said, "We want to give you a three-year contract for $3.3 million."

I said, "That's fine."

There was no negotiation. That was in the range that I expected. After all, I was only making $475,000 at the time. How could I turn it down when they were going to more than double my pay? Mr. Cooke said he was going to take care of me, and he did. I was completely satisfied.

That shows the difference between the Redskins and the Bucs. I gave the Bucs five good years and waited on them to give me a fair contract, and look what they did to me. Whereas, I played two seasons with the Redskins and still had a year left on my contract, and they came through for me. That's the difference between a great organization and a Mickey Mouse club. That's why the Redskins will always be winners and the Bucs will always be losers.

It was a good feeling to be a starter going into the 1988 season. It showed the kind of confidence Coach Gibbs had in me. Another thing that demonstrated his belief in me was trading Jay Schroeder to the Raiders. That was the same deal they were going to make with me less than a year earlier, so it was obvious they were happy with me as their quarterback. They felt I was the one to lead the team back to the Super Bowl.

At the start of the season, we had high hopes for another great year. It looked like we had everything necessary to get back into the playoffs. With the talent we had on that team, and just coming off our

Super Bowl victory, I don't think you could have convinced anyone on the team that we wouldn't be back in the playoffs.

I'm not really sure what went wrong. Anybody can sit around and make excuses, but there were no simple answers. I think you have to give a lot of credit to the people we were playing. They played hard, and they beat our behind. We were the champions, and everyone was coming after us. It seemed like most of the teams we played were waiting to ambush us. We were on the defensive all year. Of course, we didn't play well, either. We made plenty of turnovers and didn't get the ball back. At times, we didn't play good defense, and at other times, we didn't play good offense.

Right after our second game, I got what I thought was a bad stomach ache on my off day. I just laid around the house hoping it would go away, but it didn't. The next day, I saw our trainer before practice and told him my right side was hurting. He said I needed to see the team doctor. The doctor showed up before practice and wanted to examine me right then. But I told him, "No, I want to go to practice. Let's do it tonight."

So I went out and practiced all afternoon, even though my side was still aching. When I went to see the doctor later, he started pressing on my side, and it hurt every place he touched. That's when he said, "Do me a favor, Doug. Why don't you ride to the hospital with me."

"What for?" I said, "I don't really want to go to the hospital."

"Just for some observation," he answered.

Once I got to the hospital, Dr. Todd Arcomondo ran some tests on me. After he studied the results, he told me that I had to have an appendectomy right away. It was about seven o'clock at night when they operated. They said my appendix probably would have ruptured in another day.

It was a terrible feeling to be told you had to sit out four to five weeks. All the work I had done in training camp was wasted. I knew I had to start all over again. But I got in shape and was back in four weeks. It was probably too soon for me to play again.

That's when the Doug Williams Rule came into being. Some of the media started calling it that, because up until then, Coach Gibbs had a rule that a starter could not lose his position by injury. When Schroeder had been injured in 1987, he came back and was the starter again. Coach Gibbs made it absolutely clear that you couldn't lose your starting job because of an injury. But when I came back from the appendectomy, that had changed. Mark Rypien remained the starter. So they called it the Doug Williams Rule.

I didn't let it get to me or get angry about it. That's life, and you have to deal with things like that. I've been dealing with those things all of my life, so it was nothing new. It was another case of the Golden Rule. Whoever's got the gold makes the rules. And Coach Gibbs had the gold.

It turned out that Ryp hurt his shoulder the week I came back anyway, so I had to play. The next week, we went to Houston, and the Oilers beat us like we had stolen a government mule. They beat us like a drum. So Coach Gibbs thought I might have come back from surgery too quickly, and he made another quarterback change. Ryp started most of the season. Then he had a bad game against the Philadelphia Eagles, and I came off the bench to lead us to a win. I then started the last game of the season against Dallas. Coach Gibbs said the quarterback job was open going into the next season.

To finish 7-9 that year was probably the most disappointing thing that's ever happened to me in football. Even when I was in Tampa, we never experienced anything to compare to that. We had seasons with more losses, but we never went from the very top of the league to a losing season. I mean you're talking about the Super Bowl champions finishing 7-9. It was particularly hard to take, because we knew we should have had another big year. Nothing seemed to work for us.

During that season, Lisa and I were back together. Our marriage seemed to be working for a while. Lisa got pregnant, and it looked like we had worked things out. Everything was going pretty well after the Super Bowl. I guess she enjoyed being married to the Super Bowl MVP. That was something else she could show off.

The strange thing about Lisa was she didn't like the fact that I have so many friends. I basically try to get along with everybody, and Lisa has never been able to do that. It bothered her that I liked to have a lot of friends and family around me. I just like people. Someone is always calling me to do something or just to talk. Most of the time I spend at home, I'm on the phone or somebody is visiting me.

Lisa didn't grow up in a very happy environment. Her family was not close like mine. My brothers and sisters are very close-knit, and naturally we like to spend time together. And it's the same way with my close friends. People like Ricky Grant and Alonzo Shanklin. She tried to say they just hung around me because I have money. Well, Ricky and I have been friends for years. We were roommates in college, and I didn't have any money back then. That shows her mentality. She was just jealous of my friends.

We had the ongoing problem with money, too. Lisa still wanted to get more money to spend. She also didn't want to stay in Zachary. So it wasn't long before things were back to normal, and we weren't getting along.

Our son, Adrian, was born on December 2, 1988. It seemed like Lisa was enjoying staying home with the baby and being a mother. But that was probably an act, too. It wasn't long before she was complaining about things again. The marriage just wasn't working out.

In May, I had to go to Washington for a weekend on business. Before I left, we sat down and talked about splitting up. What we agreed to do was wait until Adrian was at least a year old. We agreed we would work something out then, and she said that was fine. Little did I know she had been to a lawyer and had already planned to leave for Atlanta. She was just trying to find out if I knew anything. That's the way Lisa operated.

She had already put down a deposit on an apartment. I remember she had visited a friend in Atlanta a couple of times, but I didn't think anything of it at the time. I figured she wanted to see her friend. But all the time, she was setting up her escape to Atlanta.

When I left for D.C., Lisa called Supreme Beauty and got them to send the $75,000 check that they owed me. She forged my signature on the check and went to the bank. She paid off a car note for $34,000, left $10,000 in the account and took $31,000 in cash with her. Then she packed up Adrian and her things and drove away to Atlanta in our Mercedes.

Lisa just wanted to try to hurt me. She knows I'm a conservative person. If there's anything I can't stand, it's for someone to mess with my baby or my money. Lisa knew what she was doing. She realized that part of it would get to me. Everything she did was designed to attack me in a way that she thought would hurt me the most.

By signing my name to that check, Lisa committed forgery, and I wasn't going to let her get away with stealing my money. So I pressed charges against her. Later, I dropped the charges as part of our divorce agreement.

I'll tell you why Lisa took the money. She just did what her mother had done to her father. When her mother left her father, she went and took $50,000 out of the bank and ran up her husband's credit cards, leaving him holding the bag. He had no money left in the bank and an unknown amount of debt on the credit cards. Lisa used to talk about that all the time, so she just did what Momma had taught her.

What bothered me was the way it was done. I think if you've got a problem like that, you should sit down and work it out. If you want a divorce, you should say, "This is what I want to do." I don't think you should wait until the middle of the night and sneak out. I lost a lot of respect for her Daddy, because he came to my house in the middle of the night and packed all of her things. I think that's mighty low to go to another man's house and clear things out. I don't care if it's his daughter or not. He should have at least called me and let me know what he was doing. That bothered me, because I had defended him during the time when Lisa's mother didn't even want him to be at the wedding.

It never had to become such a nasty ordeal. If it had been handled properly, we could have settled the divorce and gotten on with our lives with no hard feelings. But by doing what she did, Lisa made it a public event. Any time an athlete is involved in something like a divorce, the media jumps all over it. If it had been the average guy on the street, there never would have been a word written about it. Lisa also tried to tear down the image that I had in Washington and Louisiana. She just wanted to attack me any way she could. It's a shame, too, because she knows I'm a role model for a lot of kids. But she still wanted to try to discredit me.

It was tough to go through all that stuff. The sad part is it never had to happen. It would have been fine with me if Lisa had just said, "Doug, I'm gone." I would have made sure she was taken care of and the baby was taken care of. That wouldn't have been a problem with me. Adrian is my son, and I want to make sure he gets everything he needs. I was glad to set up a college fund for him. I went out and bought $30,000 worth of zero coupons and municipal bonds to make sure he'll have the money to go to college when he gets ready.

The downfall of our marriage was the same problems we had from the very start. Lisa wanted to control all my money, and she wanted to be in the spotlight all the time. That's not the kind of wife I wanted. I wanted Lisa to be a woman who was pushing me, not leading me. When the cameras were rolling, Lisa was always out front. That's what she liked. And I wasn't looking for that type of wife. I always wanted the kind of young lady who would encourage me and be there for me and the family. But that wasn't what Lisa wanted. She had to be the star.

The end of this marriage wasn't nearly as tough to deal with as my first one. I would still be married to Janice if she was alive. Obviously, that was something I couldn't control. I ended the second marriage by choice. So it was much easier to accept and deal with. I haven't had any trouble adjusting at all. The only thing I hate is Lisa has total control of Adrian, and she uses it to her advantage. She wants to make sure she dictates whatever I'm able to do with my son. To me, that's not right. I wanted Adrian to stay with me three months a year, but Lisa would only agree to three weeks.

Last January, I set it up so Adrian could come stay with me and Ashley for a week, but Lisa made it impossible. She said in order for Adrian to come to my house, she would have to come to Baton Rouge and stay at a hotel for three nights to make sure he was eating right and adjusting. I'm the boy's father. What does she think I'm going to do with him? She's trying to say I don't know how to take care of my own son. It's just another way of trying to get at me.

It's a shame that I will not be able to spend as much time with Adrian as I want, but I'm not going to allow Lisa to manipulate me. With the way society is today and all the problems that young black kids have, I can't believe that Lisa could not be open-minded and put Adrian's interests first. I can't believe she would not say, ''Doug, I want you to be with your son as much as possible.'' Adrian is the most important person in this whole thing. The hell with me and Lisa. But she wants to make sure she's in control and holding whatever she possibly can over my head. This really hurts Adrian, and it's going to get worse as he gets older. I hate the fact that we're not together more. I hate that he and Ashley aren't getting a chance to spend much of their growing up years together. Everything Lisa is doing in that way is detrimental to our son.

While I was going through the divorce, I was trying to get in shape for the 1989 season and ended up hurting my back. Actually, it was an aggravation of an old injury. I first hurt my back when we were playing the Los Angeles Rams in a Monday Night game in 1987. I dove in the corner of the end zone for a TD, and strained something in my back. Then it went out completely during practice on Thanksgiving Day. I was the starter at the time, but couldn't play that week.

The back injury flared up again at mini-camp in May of last year and again while I was working out at my house. That was part of my offseason training program. It wasn't really that painful at first. I just felt a little twinge in my hamstring area. I learned later that it was a disc pressing up against the sciatic nerve. Since it didn't seem to be anything serious, I still tried to work out. As an athlete, you think, "This is just a little sting. It will go away if you work it out." But it just wouldn't go away. It continued to linger.

When I went to camp, I couldn't even throw a pass. That was disappointing because Mark Rypien and I were going to compete for the starting job, and I felt like I would get it. The Redskins had another talented team, and we were hungry for a good season after what happened the previous year. Things looked very promising for the team, and I naturally wanted to be part of it.

The team doctors checked me out and thought it was a back problem, but they didn't know how serious it was. So they put me through all sorts of tests, CAT scans and MRIs. Then they decided to try traction, so I was in traction for ten days. That didn't help, so they finally did a molegram and shot that die into me. The pictures indicated the L-5 disc was pressing up against the sciatic nerve and had to be trimmed. That was the only way to relieve the pain, and it meant I had to have surgery.

A lot of people said it was career-threatening surgery, but I never looked at it that way. I conferred with my doctor, Bruce Ammerman, and he told me that I could probably come back from it. All I needed was his confidence. He was doing the surgery. I already had confidence in myself that I could come back if it was at all possible.

Dr. Ammerman is just a great guy, and he always treated me as a patient, not a football player. His main concern was my health. He wanted to make sure I could function outside football, and if I could play again, that was fine.

It was a very delicate operation. Anytime you're dealing with the spinal cord, it's extremely dangerous. It takes great skill to be able to perform surgery like I was having.

My mother and Ashley flew up to Washington to be with me. Herb Nelson, Suzanne Mayo and my cousin Robert Perkins were also there with me in the hospital. The surgery lasted a couple hours and was successful. They went in and did exactly what needed to be done, and the disc problem was corrected. I was glad to have that taken care of, but I had ten weeks of rehab ahead of me. There was no guarantee that I would play at all that season.

It was tough coming back. I was in the hospital for seven days and was flat on my back for two weeks. I couldn't bend over. I couldn't sit up for more than thirty minutes. It was really tough. I really had to work hard to get back to the team in ten weeks. I knew it would have been better for my physical well being not to come back at all in 1989, but I wanted to try to help the Redskins. There was a lot of pain, but you get used to that. As a professional athlete, you have to deal with pain most of the time.

While I was rehabilitating my back, there were some other things going on that I had deal with. My father was real sick during the fall, and he didn't seem to be getting better. Then the media tried to make a big deal out of a question concerning my salary.

The Redskins wanted to put me on the non-football-related injury list. But they knew I hurt my back getting ready for the season. I talked to Mr. Cooke before I had surgery, and I knew everything would be taken care of. I was never worried about not getting paid. But the media came out with stories saying that Doug Williams was going to get the players union to sue the Redskins. I never even talked to the players union about a lawsuit. I always got my pay check from the Redskins, just like I knew I would. I got the full $1.1 million for the season.

Meanwhile, my father went into the hospital in October suffering from pneumonia. Daddy had been through so much before, and I really thought he would come out of this, too. But the longer he was in the hospital, the worse he got. Then after about three weeks, he slipped into a coma. He wasn't very strong at that point, because he had lost so much fluid from the pneumonia. Later on, they discovered he had bone cancer. So I knew he was critical.

About that time, I was finally able to come back to the team. Mentally and physically, that was probably the most difficult time of my life. I had to try to get ready to play, and they named me the starter against Dallas in my first game back.

That same morning, I called Daddy's hospital room, and my brother Larry answered the phone. I asked him how Daddy was doing, and he said, "Daddy left us."

I didn't understand what Larry was saying. Then he said, "He died." I couldn't say anything after that. I just held the phone for a minute. Then I hung up and went outside and cried. I had to get it out. After a while I was able to go back inside and get ready for practice. I practiced the whole day without telling many people about it. The media didn't know, because I didn't want to make a big deal out of a personal thing.

I knew my father would have wanted me to play, because he had encouraged me so much during my rehab. He was looking forward to me coming back and knew that I had worked hard for it. I was sure he would have preferred that I play the game, instead of coming right home. I also talked to M'Dear about it, and she told me, "Baby, you might as well stay up there and play, because you've done all you can do for your Daddy. And he would have wanted you to play." That was all I needed to hear, so I went ahead and got ready to play. The funeral was scheduled for the Tuesday after the Dallas game.

The toughest thing about returning to play so soon was taking the physical beating that you get as a quarterback. I hadn't been able to do anything in training camp, so I wasn't physically prepared for the pounding I got.

I played against Dallas, and every time I got hit, some of my teammates and coaches cringed. But I was all right. I took some hits and got right back up. That was the only good thing about the game. Nothing happened for us offensively or defensively. Nobody played football that night. A lot of the media said the team was flat. I don't know how you can measure something like that. We just didn't play well that night. Football is a team game that involves individuals, and you never know what your teammate is thinking or going through on a particular day. You just hope he plays up to par. On that night, we as a team did not play up to par.

The next week, I started again. We were playing at Philadelphia against one of the best defenses in the NFL. It was a tremendous defensive effort on both sides. What we did was avoid the mistakes that Philly had been capitalizing on all year. We didn't give them those opportunities, and we kept the ball away from them. We made first downs when we had to, and the defense held when it had to. That's how we won the game—a great win for our team.

Any time you play the Eagles, you expect to get hit, and I did. You're talking about the best defensive line in football. They got to me a whole bunch of times. But I threw the ball away and took the hit rather than being sacked. You're going to pay a price when you play the Eagles, but it makes it a little easier when you win.

After we beat the Eagles, I really thought things were looking good for the team and for me. To withstand the assault they gave me and to get up and walk away was really important. I felt fine after the game, but a couple of days later, I began to feel the pain.

That Tuesday, my hip started to ache again, right where it had hurt in the summer. It was the sciatic nerve again. All the hits I took had irritated the nerve. I just wasn't able to move, so I told Coach Gibbs that I couldn't practice. I was just too sore. Coach Gibbs told me if I couldn't practice, he was going to go with Rypien. So Ryp returned as the starter, and I was the backup for the rest of the season.

If they had let me stay out of contact for a week, I think I would have been able to play again and play well. My hip hurt bad on Tuesday, Wednesday and Thursday, but it was getting better by Friday and was fine by Saturday. But I wasn't given the opportunity to play. I guess it was the Doug Williams Rule again.

It was hard to go back to the bench, but I accepted it. I don't make those decisions, and I just have to live with them. I've learned to adjust to anything. After all, what else are you going to do? You have to adjust.

We finally got things going our way late in the year. We won our last five games and just missed making the playoffs. I think if we had gotten into the playoffs, we could have beaten some teams.

Ryp was the starter and played pretty well during the late stretch when we were winning. So I wasn't surprised when Coach Gibbs came out and said Ryp would be the starter going into training camp; it was expected. But I also expected to be in camp with him.

I'm disappointed not being part of the Redskins. But I'm a very content person. As long as nobody is doing anything to me mentally or physically, I'm not going to complain. I've had eleven good years of pro football. I've accomplished things that nobody else has accomplished. I've got a Super Bowl ring and I can still walk around. That's not bad. I feel pretty good about my football career.

• *17*

You're a Great Competitor

The drum beats for everyone. It's important for every pro athlete to realize that. No matter who you are, there's going to come a time when your career is over and you'd better be ready for it. The drum beat for me. And it's going to beat for Joe Montana and Lawrence Taylor and Michael Jordan and Magic Johnson. They're going to hear their tunes, too. That's the way it is.

I've always tried to prepare myself mentally to accept whatever happens. Anytime you play football as long as I have, you've seen plenty of players get released. You come to understand it's just part of the game.

It would have been nice to play another year for the Redskins, but I'm not going to feel sorry for myself. Football has been good to me. It's been better to me than most. I always had a goal of playing ten years in the NFL, and it looks like I'll come up a year short. But it's like the old saying, "Shoot for the moon and if you don't make it, you'll still land in the stars." If I don't get a chance to play that tenth season, I still landed in the stars. I'm still in the solar system. How can I be disappointed with what I've done? If I had only played one or two years, that would have been a major disappointment. But I played nine years in the NFL and two in the USFL. So I had eleven years as a professional. I'll take that.

What I'll miss most is being around the guys and being involved in the competition. But there will be plenty of things I won't miss. I'm not going to miss training camp. I'm not going to miss it when it gets freezing cold. I'm not going miss the city-to-city excursions. In today and out tomorrow—I never liked that.

Of course, it will be hard to get used to not getting ready to play every week. I'll miss not preparing to go into battle. It's competition, and I've been doing it since I was eight years old. You're talking about twenty-seven years of getting ready to go out to war every week. And all of a sudden you don't have to do that any more. That will be something I'll have to adjust to.

Pro football has been very rewarding for me. It's given me a headstart financially. I've been able to do things for myself, for my family and for others. I've been able to open some doors for other people, and that's the best aspect of it. Football has also given me a chance to meet so many people that I would never have known. And I've traveled to places that I probably wouldn't have seen. It was an exciting experience.

My career was filled with ups and downs. I had some great years in Tampa and Washington, and I had some tough years. Injuries were always a factor. I had to play with great pain for much of my career, and there's been tremendous adversity and controversy throughout my playing days. It was not easy being a black quarterback in the NFL. It may never be. But if I had to weigh the good against the bad, the good would outweigh the bad. I've been able to do some things that other people only dream about.

If football is over for me, I want to take some time off and enjoy life. I'd like to be in a position where time is not a concern, in that you don't always have to be at a certain place at a certain time. I don't know what it's like to have spare time. I've been playing football for so long that I need a break. This will give me a chance to spend time with my family and friends. I can go to high school and college football games and I can watch pro games on television. I'll really enjoy that. I'm not only a player, I'm a fan. I love the game, and I want to stay in it as a coach.

I'm fortunate that I don't have to run out and find a job. Financially, I'm able to take off as much time as I want. But it's not about that. I want to work. I really want to be around kids and help them in their careers. It's important for me to become a coach. I want to be in a situation where I can share what I've learned and teach kids what it's going to take to get where they want to be. I know I can help a lot of people in coaching.

But there will be other opportunities for me, too. After I got released by the Redskins, one of the first people to call me was Mark Van Grack, who owns the sports apparel business with which I'm affiliated. He said, "Well, now you can come to work full-time for us." I was also contacted about working for the NFL in a program that counsels college players, and there's a possibility I could become a scout. There are going to be a lot of opportunities opening up for me, because I've been fortunate enough to work with people during my career. It's not so much what you do on the field that people remember. What really leaves an impression is what you did in your free time and during the offseason. The average fan isn't going to remember a player unless he did something to touch his life. A person will remember you more for standing there for two hours signing autographs for kids than for throwing an eighty-yard touchdown pass.

I've had a great career in professional football, but I know there's much more out there for me to do. Some players have trouble adjusting to being out of football because they haven't prepared themselves for it. I've been ready to retire. I got my degree and then spent some time teaching and coaching. I'm well prepared to start a career in coaching.

What I'm probably going to do is become a coach at a small college. I don't want to coach on the professional level. There's too much bullshit and politics that goes on in the NFL. Like Bobby Mitchell of the Redskins said, coaching on the professional level is the good ol' boy system. It's who you know, not what you can do. I don't want to involve myself in that.

Think about the way coaches go from one team to another. Jerry Glanville gets fired in Houston, and he goes to Atlanta in a heartbeat. It's just the good ol' boy system.

If a team loses a coach, the general manager calls his buddy on another team and says, "Hello, pal, who's coaching your running backs?"

"You need somebody. Why don't you hire this guy."

"Oh, he's your boy. Then I'll look after him."

The NFL is a clique. You've got to know the right people to move up in the league. Everything is based on who you know. To me, that's no way to operate a business.

I'd like to coach at a small college because I want to be able to go into the homes and share some of my experiences with the kids and parents. I want them to know that I'll make myself available to them. I'll be there when they have a problem. I want to help those kids grow up. I want to help make them a better person, a good athlete and a college graduate. A lot of people helped me along those lines, and I feel I owe it to the youngsters to help them. Pro football was just icing on the cake. Now I can become a coach like my brother, Robert.

I haven't made any specific plans, because my football career may not be over yet. But I'm sure if I decided to retire today, I would get some calls. One of my good friends and former teammates, Dwight Scales, just got the head coaching job at Morehouse College. That's the type of small college I prefer. I don't want to deal with the multimillion-dollar programs. I don't want to negotiate a $20 million TV contract like Notre Dame got. The hustle and bustle of major college football isn't for me.

Before I went to the Redskins, I had an opportunity to coach at Bishop College. But I turned it down, because I had a chance to stay home and coach at Southern University. So I'm sure there will be some openings when the time comes.

Wherever I end up coaching, I want to be able to recruit some good student-athletes. I'll talk to the kids about what they want to do with their lives. To be honest with you, if they just want to play football, I don't want them to play for me.

I want to be around young people who are interested in getting an education. As long as they'll make the effort to get the work done, I'll be right there working with them. I want to teach young people what it's like to be a competitor, what it's like to be a student, what it's like to grow up in America and how to survive here. I want them to treat football like a survival course. You're out on the field to survive. This is how you earn your scholarship. That scholarship allows you to receive an education, and that education will allow you to survive, thrive and succeed. When you take that approach, it makes you a better competitor and a stronger person. It prepares you for life.

Most of the things I'll do as a coach will be patterned after what

Coach Robinson does at Grambling. I've been fortunate to have been graced with Coach Rob's presence in my life. I feel like I'm the luckiest man in the world to have played for him.

Without a doubt, I'd love to coach at Grambling some day. I bleed black and gold. Grambling is a part of me. But there's another part of me that would like to go to Southern University, because I'd be at home. Those two places are closest to my heart. I'd go to either one in a heartbeat. But I may never get that chance, so I'm ready to go wherever there's an opportunity to coach.

Becoming a coach is not a matter of money—I'm in pretty good shape financially for an ol' country boy. It doesn't take that much money to live in Zachary. If I was living in New York City or some other big city like that, I might be a little scared. But I've got my house in Zachary paid for, and I'm not a big spender, so I don't need too much. I know I'll be very content with whatever I have and whatever I'm doing in life.

One thing I'd like to see in my lifetime is the end of the black quarterback syndrome. What's sad is the game hasn't changed that much as far as giving black quarterbacks a chance to play. You look at Randall Cunningham, and he was a cinch. He had to play in the league. Then Warren Moon provides that same thing. He's proved he can perform in the NFL. Andre Ware won the Heisman Trophy, so he had to be drafted early. Those kind of guys cannot be overlooked. You can't hide guys like them. You can't just put them on the shelf somewhere. They have to play because there aren't many who can do the job like they can. But there are so many other black quarterbacks who should get a chance to play, too.

The only way the NFL can continue to keep black quarterbacks down is to deny them a fair opportunity to develop. What I mean by that is putting time and effort into that guy's development and treating him just like any other young quarterback. Look at guys like Major Harris and Tony Rice, I'm sure if someone had worked with them and given them the attention that young white quarterbacks get, they could have made it in the league. But they're not going to get that chance.

I hope it's not too long before another black quarterback plays in the Super Bowl. I'd like to do it again. I pulled for Randall and Warren to make it last season. I think they're both close to making it, but their teams are so up and down that you never know which one is going to show up. If Philadelphia gets a couple more weapons, they could make it. They just need another good receiver and maybe another good offensive lineman. They've already got the defense. So they've got a shot at becoming a Super Bowl-caliber team. Warren's road doesn't look as smooth. I don't know what's going to happen to the Oilers, so it might be hard for them to get there. If you go by the law of averages, it will probably be quite awhile before there's another black quarterback in the Super Bowl. But I didn't really think John Elway and the Broncos would ever get back to the Super Bowl, and they did it this year. So anything is possible.

But it's going to take more than both Randall and Moon playing in the Super Bowl for there to be equality for black quarterbacks in the National Football League. How many black quarterbacks are there now in the league? Randall, Warren, Rodney Peete, Don McPherson and Andre Ware. That's it. There are probably eighty to eighty-five quarterbacks in the NFL, and only five are black. I think that says it all. A lot of people with closed minds in the NFL don't want to give black quarterbacks a fair shot, and nothing is going to change their attitude. I know I didn't. And whatever Randall and Warren and Andre Ware do isn't going to change their way of thinking. It's going to take new leaders with open minds.

Things won't be on an equitable basis until there are proportionate numbers of black NFL quarterbacks to the population of black people in this country. That means about 20 percent of the quarterbacks in the league should be black. And maybe more than that. When we start seeing twenty or twenty-five black quarterbacks playing in the NFL, then we'll know the syndrome is over. But I don't really think I'll live long enough to see that. My daughter and my son might see it. It's going to be awhile, believe me.

As for my contributions, I just want to be remembered as a competitor. I hope people will always think of Doug Williams as a guy who gave everything he had whenever he put on that helmet—and kept giving it all to the very end. I felt like I never lost, regardless of the score, because when you give it all, that's all you can give. I don't want to be remembered as the great black quarterback. That's putting me into one category. I'd like to be remembered as a true competitor in the National Football League.

I'm very satisfied with what I've been able to accomplish in football. Really, there's nothing more that I can do that I haven't already done. There are some Hall of Fame quarterbacks who haven't accomplished what I've accomplished. I've got a Super Bowl ring. Fran Tarkenton doesn't have one. Don Fouts doesn't have one. John Elway doesn't have one. I could go on and on.

In sports, your first goal is always to bring that championship banner home with you. Michael Jordan isn't out there playing basketball for the MVP award. He wants to win the world championship. It's the same way in football. I didn't care how many touchdown passes I threw as long as we won. The only thing that I ever played for was the championship. Winning the Super Bowl was the ultimate accomplishment in my career. There could never be anything to top that.

What does it require for a quarterback to get into the Hall of Fame? If you measure what a quarterback really does for his team and what he's accomplished for that team, then I should get into the Hall of Fame. But if you go by the yardstick and stats and numbers, I probably won't get in. That just happens to be how they usually measure things in football.

Look at what I've done with the Bucs and Redskins. I've been in the playoffs five times, I've been on three division winning teams, I've been to the NFC championship game three times, and my team won the Super Bowl and I was named the Super Bowl MVP. That would probably get most quarterbacks into the Hall of Fame. I think it should. But it all depends on how you measure success. I don't have the stats that some other quarterbacks have; I've always sacrificed my stats to help my team win. That should be considered in determining someone's accomplishments. If you measure it by leadership, overcoming obstacles, being durable and those types of things, I would make it.

I believe in giving everything you've got to give in order for your team to be successful, whether it's being a leader or going out there and giving up your body. It's all for the team. If the players I've played against over the years were voting for the Hall of Fame, I'd make it. They respect me and understand what I've done for my teams. In my heart, I feel that I belong in the Hall of Fame. But I don't think it will happen. I don't even think my name will ever come up.

No matter what happens from here on out, I can't imagine receiving a compliment greater than the one I received from Bill Walsh in 1988. We played the 49ers out in San Francisco in a Monday Night game, and they beat us in what was probably the turning point of their Super Bowl season. After the game, I was standing out on the field talking to Joe Montana, and Bill Walsh was running toward their locker room. But Coach Walsh came over, shook my hand and said, ''Doug, I just want to let you know I think you're a great competitor.'' To come from Bill Walsh, that was everything. It really meant so much. He didn't have to go out of his way to speak to me. He didn't have to tell me that. But he thought enough of me to say something like that.

To me, being a competitor and earning the respect of your peers is the greatest achievement any football player can ever have.

My Stats

If you've read this far, you know my feelings about quarterback statistics: they don't tell the whole story. When the going is tough, the quarterback who takes a sack rather than an incomplete pass only looks good on paper after the season. But his team may wind up out of field goal range, or in a poor position for the punt.

There have been plenty of passes I have thrown that were placed so that one man and one man alone—my receiver—could catch it. If he didn't, tough. We'd go get them next down. But there'd be no interception. And there'd be no sack. Just an incomplete pass on my stats.

But I'm not embarrassed about my statistics. On the pages that follow, I've included excerpts taken from the 1989 press guide of the Washington Redskins, and also my yearly statistics and career bests. I think these stats aren't too shabby. But you decide.

College: Doug was named first-team All-America quarterback by the Associated Press in 1977, his senior year at Grambling. He finished fourth in the Heisman Trophy voting. He was named MVP of the East-West Shrine game and impressed scouts in the Senior Bowl. He posted a 35-5 record as a starter at Grambling, throwing for 8,411 yards and 93 touchdowns, an NCAA record. He threw a touchdown pass in every game but one. Doug was voted the Louisiana College Athlete of the Year in 1977.

1978: Doug was drafted in the first round (17th pick overall) by the Tampa Bay Buccaneers. He was a unanimous choice for the NFL All-Rookie team. He started ten games, one of which (against New Orleans, December 17) he played with his broken jaw wired shut. Doug missed six games because of injuries, five because of the broken jaw, which he suffered in the tenth game against the Los Angeles Rams. The Bucs were 4-4 in games that Doug played from start to finish.

1979: Doug joined an elite group of quarterbacks when he led his team to a conference championship game in one of his first two seasons. He was sacked only seven times in 404 pass attempts.

1980: Doug was selected the team's Most Valuable Player by a number of local groups, including the *St. Petersburg Times*. He threw for 300 or more yards in four games. He threw a team record four touchdown passes against Minnesota.

1981: In his final four games of the regular season, Doug led the Bucs to the playoffs by completing 60.7 percent of his passes for 1,048 yards, six touchdowns and three interceptions. He finished the season with a 76.5 quarterback rating, the third best in his career. He completed nine passes that were longer than fifty yards, seven for touchdowns. He again was selected the Bucs Most Valuable Player by the *St. Petersburg Times*.

1982: Doug threw for more than 190 yards in eight of nine games in his last season with the Bucs. His 53.4 completion percentage was the highest in his tenure with Tampa. He completed twenty or more passes in five of nine games. Bothered by a sore knee most of the year, he underwent arthroscopic surgery following the season. Doug finished his career in Tampa with a 33-31-1 record and was the starting quarterback in thirty-three of the Bucs' first thirty-six NFL victories.

1983-85: Doug signed with the Oklahoma Outlaws of the United States Football League in September of 1983 and played two seasons, in the spring of 1984 and 1985. He played fifteen games in 1984 before a knee injury sidelined him for the season. His best game in the USFL came in that first season against New Jersey, May 6, 1984, when he completed 31 of 51 passes for 381 yards and one touchdown. Doug moved with the franchise to Arizona the following season and threw for more than 300 yards in five games.

1986: Doug signed with Washington as a free agent after the USFL folded and served as a backup to Jay Schroeder. He played briefly in only one game, against Dallas, and threw one incomplete pass.

1987: Doug was the subject of trade rumors as the season began but finished the year at the pinnacle of his profession; he was named the MVP of Super bowl XXII. Doug set four Super Bowl records in the Redskins 42-10 victory over Denver, Jan. 31, 1987: most yards passing in a game (340), most yards passing in a quarter (228), most touchdown passes (4), and longest completion (80 yards). Doug started the season as Schroeder's backup but was pressed into action on the ninth play of the season opener, against Philadelphia, when Schroeder suffered a sprained shoulder. He started the following week against Atlanta, then gave way to Schroeder when players returned from the strike. Doug received his second chance of the season in Week 9 against Detroit when he relieved a struggling Schroeder early in the first half. He led Washington to a 20-13 victory and earned his second start of the season the following week against the Rams. Doug suffered his second loss as a starter against L.A., but was scheduled to start the next week against the Giants before he suffered a sprained back during practice on Thanksgiving Day. Because the Redskins were winning with Schroeder, Doug sat on the bench until the regular-season finale, when he again answered the relief call. He entered Game 15 against Minnesota in the third quarter and rallied Washington to a 27-24 victory. That performance earned him the starting role in the playoffs and the Redskins won three games to capture the world championship.

1988: When team trainers and a selected group of veterans met to choose the Redskins' recipient of the 1988 Ed Block Courage Award, they didn't take long to reach a decision. Williams was the obvious choice. Doug has overcome obstacle after obstacle throughout his career, and last season [1988] was no exception. Although he proved wrong all the skeptics who predicted that his wearing knees wouldn't hold up through a sixteen-game season, Doug couldn't avoid an appendicitis attack that placed him on injured reserve from Games 4 to 7. Williams' replacement, Mark Rypien, suffered bruised ribs four weeks after taking over at quarterback. The Redskins needed Doug to start against Green Bay, only four and a half weeks after his operation, and Doug played the entire game against the Packers and led Washington to a 20-17 victory. "Doug is as fierce of a competitor as there is," coach Joe Gibbs said. "I think what he gives us is a guy who leads by example. He's someone who the younger players can look up to. He's been through a lot and he's overcome a lot. He'll do whatever he has to do to help the team." Doug helped the Redskins as both a starter and a reliever last season. He rallied the team three times in the fourth quarter when it needed two scores to win. He raised his relief record with Washington to 4-0 (3-0 in 1987, 1-0 in 1988) in Week 14 in Philadelphia when he came off the bench twice to relieve Rypien, who bruised his right thumb early in the first half. With Washington trailing 19-10 late in the third quarter, Doug directed three scoring drives—one for a third-quarter field goal, another that ended with a two-yard touchdown pass to Terry Orr, and the third that culminated in a game-winning, forty-four-yard field goal with one second remaining. As a starter, Doug posted a 4-6 record but his offense was without a consistent running game most of the season. In the two games in which the Redskins have run the ball the best over the past two seasons with Doug at quarterback—in Super Bowl XXII when the Redskins rushed for 280 yards versus Denver and in Game 16 last season against Cincinnati when they ran for 166 yards—Williams' combined statistics are 35 of 51 for 557 yards, six touchdowns and two interceptions. Even without a consistent running game last season, Williams and Rypien combined for the most touchdown passes

(33) and the most passing yards (4,339) in the league. They combined to set team records for net passing yardage (4,136), attempts (592), completions (327), passing first downs (202), and touchdown passes (33). But Doug's biggest contribution couldn't be measured by statistics. His attitude, leadership ability, and determination to overcome adversity made him one of the most valuable players on the team.

CAREER STATISTICS

Year	Team	Att	Comp	Yds	Passing Pct	TD	Int	Rating	Rushing No	Yds	TD
1978	Tampa Bay	194	73	1170	37.6	7	8	53.5	27	23	1
1979	Tampa Bay	397	166	2448	41.8	18	24	52.6	35	119	2
1980	Tampa Bay	521	254	3396	48.8	20	16	69.7	58	370	4
1981	Tampa Bay	471	238	3563	50.5	19	14	76.5	48	209	4
1982	Tampa Bay	307	164	2071	53.4	9	11	69.4	35	158	4
1986	Washington	1	0	0	0.0	0	0	39.6	0	0	0
1987	Washington	143	81	1156	56.0	11	5	94.0	7	9	1
1988	Washington	380	213	2609	56.1	15	12	77.4	9	0	1
1989	Washington	93	51	585	54.8	1	3	64.1	1	-4	0
NFL Totals		2507	1240	17088	49.2	100	93	66.2	220	883	15

USFL

Year	Team	Att	Comp	Yds	Passing Pct	TD	Int	Rating	Rushing No	Yds	TD
1984	Oklahoma	528	261	3084	49.4	15	21	60.5	28	89	3
1985	Arizona	509	271	3673	53.2	21	17	72.1	27	82	1
Totals		1037	532	6757	51.3	36	38	68.3	47	171	4

PLAYOFF STATISTICS

Team	Att	Comp	Yds	Passing Pct	TD	Int	Rating	Rushing No	Yds	TD
Tampa Bay	85	27	444	31.8	2	9	18.8	9	28	0
Washington	84	41	666	48.8	7	2	93.5	8	4	0
Totals	169	68	1110	40.2	9	11	53.6	17	32	0

CAREER BESTS

MOST COMPLETIONS		LONGS	
30 vs Cleveland	09/28/80	84t vs Detroit	12/20/81
30 vs Pittsburgh	09/11/88	81t vs Chicago	11/01/81
30 vs Minnesota	11/16/80	80t vs Denver	01/31/88
27 vs San Francisco	11/21/88	77t vs Oakland	10/18/81
25 vs Green Bay	10/23/88	75 vs Dallas	01/02/82

CAREER BESTS

MOST YARDS		MOST ATTEMPTS	
486 vs Minnesota	11/16/80	56 vs Cleveland	09/28/80
430 vs Pittsburgh	09/11/88	55 vs Minnesota	11/16/80
367 vs Chicago	01/02/83	52 vs Pittsburgh	09/11/88
350 vs Chicago	12/20/80	50 vs NY Giants	09/05/88
343 vs Cleveland	09/28/80	49 vs Chicago	01/02/83

(Has 13 career 300-yards games)

Statistics and yearly summaries reprinted from the Washington Redskins 1989 Press Guide courtesy of the Washington Redskins.

INDEX